What people are saying about **NOISE:**

NOISE is a no-nonsense book that offers much needed relief. With her trademark passion intact, Tomeo gives readers heartfelt spiritual direction on how to make use of the media without the media remaking you.

— Raymond Arroyo
EWTN News Director & New York Times Best-Selling Author

NOISE gives a unique and important perspective on the work of the media in all its forms. In a world that has become ever more influenced by the power of the media, **NOISE** encourages us to approach the media with our faith front and center. Teresa Tomeo's work is contemporary, faith-filled, and practical.

— Cardinal Adam Maida
Archbishop of Detroit

Like Pope John Paul ll, Teresa knows how the media is a powerful tool that can be used for good or evil. She gives a comprehensive analysis of what is wrong with today's secular media and practical ways to begin to transform the media for good.

— Fr. Frank Pavone
National Director, Priests for Life

NOISE is a breathtakingly swift tour through the worlds of television, radio, Internet, advertising, and music. And when you come out the other side, you will know more about the state of modern media and what you can do about it than ninety-nine percent of your friends and acquaintances.

— Al Kresta
President/CEO, Ave Maria Radio

In **NOISE**, Broadcaster Teresa Tomeo so thoroughly documents the negative impact of media on families that no reader will be able any longer to regard TV, the Internet, radio, and video games as harmless. Especially valuable are the action items that can be used to defend children and make a difference in the media.

— Bert Ghezzi
Best-Selling Author

What people are saying about **NOISE**:

This is not only an exposé of the current situation, but is also a warning to families and a guidebook for a proper understanding and use of modern media. We should all be grateful for Teresa's profound insights and call to action.

— Steve Ray
Best-Selling Author

In a world full of distractions, **NOISE**, provides much-needed guidance for Catholic families. Teresa Tomeo gives you the tools to effectively navigate the media...all the while maintaining a sane family life.

— Pia de Solenni
CEO, Diotima Consulting

NOISE addresses an important topic in a balanced and effective way. Teresa Tomeo writes from years of experience and gives us the benefit of an "insider's" knowledge in a dynamic and easy to read style. An important contribution to an issue that affects all of us.

— Ralph Martin
President, Renewal Ministries

Teresa Tomeo gives great facts and insight into media bias and shows us how to fight back and help make changes. A must read for parents and the Action Items are fantastic!

— Janet Morana
Co-Founder, Silent No More

In my mind, there is no more credible person in the Catholic media to address this situation than Teresa Tomeo. Drawing upon her vast journalistic and investigative experience, Teresa straightforwardly makes clear just how bad the situation really is, and then, more importantly, gives us something that we can do to make it better.

— Fr. John Riccardo
Host, Christ is the Answer—*Ave Maria Radio*

11/03/07

Thomas:
God bless you!
Teresa
Tomeo

NOISE

HOW OUR MEDIA-SATURATED CULTURE
DOMINATES LIVES AND DISMANTLES FAMILIES

TERESA TOMEO

ASCENSION PRESS

West Chester, Pennsylvania

Ascension Press
Post Office Box 1990
West Chester, PA 19380
Orders: 1-800-376-0520
www.AscensionPress.com

Cover design: The Design Works Group, Inc., Sisters, Oregon

Printed in the United States of America

ISBN: 978-1-932927-94-8

This book is dedicated to:

Pope John Paul II,
For your profound Christian witness and your
incredible work in spreading the beautiful Catholic
faith. You have helped the world see that the media,
when used properly, can be a force for great good.

My husband, Dominic,
For your love, support, and unwavering faith, and
for your guidance, which brought me back home to
Rome. Next to Jesus you are the best thing that has ever
happened to me. I love you.

Contents

Acknowledgments

Many thanks to my dear friends and former broadcasting colleagues who have made a major difference in my life, in my work, and in the media, and who have gone on to be with the Lord: Gene Taylor, Steve Kay, Doc Andrews, and Phil Lamka. Thank you for your friendship, your inspiration, and your commitment to excellence in broadcasting.

To my dear friends who are working hard in today's tough mass media and entertainment climate: Bob, Katie, Ruth, Wanda, Doris, Mike, Jeff, Sandra, Steve, John, and the many others who are doing what they can to provide balance and improve content, keep the faith. Thank you for your support, courage, and convictions. We need you.

To my friends and colleagues at Ave Maria Radio. Thank you for the opportunity to witness every day on the Catholic airwaves.

To Matthew Pinto and the entire team at Ascension Press for all their untiring efforts in making this book a reality, especially Lorraine Ranalli for her many creative contributions to the manuscript.

To my family, for your encouragement, especially my parents, Rose and Mike. Thank you for the gift of my Catholic faith. I love you.

You Can't Escape the Noise

Uncertain about where she is, what day it is, or whether she is dreaming, Kathy wearily opens one eye in response to the shrill sound of voices, glancing at the bright display of the clock radio on the nightstand. It is 6:30 a.m. The incessant chatter is emanating from her alarm clock. She gives it a good whack, crawls out of bed, and stumbles to the bathroom. There she encounters her husband and the voices of impetuous news anchors delivering the day's headlines in their rapid-fire style. Kathy's husband likes to listen to the news-talk station as he begins his day, but the early-morning intrusion makes Kathy reach for the Tylenol. The sounds of a news ticker and an overly dramatic female anchor are interrupted by the calm, concerned voice of a commercial actor: *Do you suffer from a lack of desire for intimacy? XYZ Laboratories is conducting an investigational study…* "This is way too much information," Kathy blurts out as she reaches behind the shower curtain to turn the radio off. Tom, her husband, has long since vacated the bathroom. Kathy quickly brushes her teeth, washes her face, and heads back into the bedroom to change. She is hoping to have a bit of private

1

conversation with Tom before heading downstairs to fix breakfast and make lunches for their children, but she is too late. Tom barely notices his wife as he busily reviews his day's schedule on his Blackberry.

Kathy proceeds downstairs and into the kitchen. Her two younger children are perched in front of the family room TV arguing over which program to watch, seemingly unconcerned by the fact that they have to catch a school bus in mere minutes. Her oldest son is parked at the kitchen table with his head buried in his laptop. Checking e-mail, he offers a passive grunt in response to his mother's "good morning." Kathy's teenage daughter grabs everyone's attention as she enters the kitchen panicking over the fact that she may have lost the fifty new songs she had downloaded on her iPod. When they realize she is not yelling at them but rather at the cell phone that appears to have fused her right ear and shoulder together, her siblings quickly go back to their own gadgets. Tom wisps through the kitchen amidst the confusion. With his Blackberry in one hand and his briefcase in the other, he stretches his neck to give Kathy a peck on the cheek as he heads out the back door. "How about breakfast?" she calls to him in the driveway. Without missing a beat he shakes his head, opens the car door, and responds, "Already late for a meeting. Give me a rain check."

As she turns to walk back into the kitchen, Kathy is nearly knocked over by her daughter, who rushes through the doorway. "Gotta go, Ma. I'm catching a ride with Jamie. I'm going to help her set up her new computer after school, so I'll be late." With that, Kathy's daughter disappears. Her oldest son has already packed up his laptop, and the younger two are scattered about. Feeling defeated, Kathy slumps her shoulders. She looks mindlessly at the TV that has been left on in the family room and wonders when her family last had some real face time together. Although this is a typical morning in Kathy's home, she is beginning to see that the very technology which was supposed to make life simpler has actually made it more complicated.

Most of us can empathize with Kathy's situation. Because of the dramatic explosion of media outlets and personal communication devices over the past twenty years, we spend more time with our electronics than we do with each other. It is ironic that despite these advanced means of communicating, we are becoming an isolated population. The telephone has long been a substitute for physically visiting with friends. E-mail has replaced the personal touch of a handwritten letter. Children retreat from each other and their families to the privacy of their Game Boys. Teenagers who once congregated on street corners now instant message (IM) from their computers or chat via cell phones. Teens who once gathered in living rooms with their families to watch their favorite TV shows can now catch many of these same prime time programs on their cell phones, anytime and anywhere, thanks to wireless companies offering everything from MTV to NBC to Nickelodeon literally in the palm of their hands.[1]

Magazine covers, television news programs, and countless studies now regularly chronicle the media's dominance in our lives, yet we just cannot seem to get away from television, radio, the Internet, e-mail, cell phones, billboards, and magazines. TV sets are not only standard pieces of furniture in just about every room of our homes, but also in doctors' waiting rooms, restaurants, and grocery store checkout lines. The noise is more than a minor annoyance or interruption. The constant bombardment of images and messages is having a powerful impact on children, families, and marriages. Aggressive behavior, eating disorders, alcohol and drug abuse, a loss of intimacy between spouses, immorality, and the absence of God in peoples' lives can largely be attributed to media over-exposure. Our media-saturated culture is a dominant force that tears at the moral fabric of our society. As the old adage goes: *Garbage in, garbage out.* Everything we digest, orally and mentally, affects us. Well into the twenty-first century, the words of Jesus still ring true: "For out of the abundance of the heart the mouth speaks" (Matthew 12:34).

The issue of media influence has become so critical that a national conference was held in New York City in February 2007, bringing together doctors, researchers, media executives, and policymakers to examine the impact of media on young people. Organizers from Common Sense Media and the Aspen Institute said their goal was to "create the most significant national discussion on the impact of media and entertainment on kids and families."[2]

In January 2007, the Parents Television Council (PTC) stated that television violence is "alarmingly more frequent and more disturbing than ever before," citing research that indicated a seventy-five percent increase since 1998.[3] Over the last three decades, more than a thousand research studies have shown a connection between violence in the media and aggressive behavior in young people. A 2003 study conducted by researchers from the University of Michigan found that children who watch aggressive television programs are more likely to have a tendency toward violent behavior as adults.[4] A University of Kansas study found that children spend more time watching TV than doing any other activity except sleep.[5] Still more research on media influence estimates that two million Internet users are addicted to Internet pornography, with at least 200,000 spending more than eleven hours a week surfing for erotic content.[6]

There have been the shocking front-page stories on the fallout of media influence, cases such as the two boys, a ten-year-old from Texas and a nine-year-old from Pakistan, who accidentally hanged themselves after trying to emulate the hanging of Saddam Hussein, which they viewed on the evening news.[7] The vast majority of cases, though, involve the "behind closed doors" struggles of families. Such struggles with the media may never make the local news, but they are making the lives of many families miserable.

As a speaker and a talk show host, I regularly meet parents who tell me how they are in major battles for their children's souls—as well as for their own sanity—because of immoral content in music, on the Internet, radio, and prime-time TV. I hear about struggles with pornography, especially the addicting power of Internet porn, from not only teenagers, but also from couples whose marriages have been destroyed. The example most prominent in my mind is that of an attractive young woman who approached me following one of my talks. She had tears in her eyes as she thanked me for the work I was doing. Then she proceeded to tell me about her marriage. She and her husband were once the picture-perfect couple in their parish. They had a nice home, were active in the church, and had two beautiful girls. Her world began to fall apart, though, when she discovered her husband was addicted to on-line porn. She tried to get him into counseling but he refused. Out of concern for her children, the two separated. Shortly after her husband moved out, she discovered that her two girls may have been exposed to some pornographic material on the Internet because the family computer was in the girls' bedroom. Her husband would sneak into their room at night to view vile images while the girls were sleeping.

Whether by chance or by choice, today's kids—armed with technology they first learned to use in preschool and kindergarten—are entering into dark places for which they are not prepared. Even tech-savvy older children are little match for pedophiles and other thugs who are looking for easy targets. Teens and pre-teens are often too trusting, naïve, and desperate for personal attention. In wanting to meet up with kids their own age, they think nothing of posting personal information on the Internet. Though teens use their own cryptic language, predators are quick studies who learn the vocabulary of their prey. PIR ("parent in room"), POS ("parent over shoulder"), ASL ("age, sex, location"), CU ("see you"), EG ("evil grin"), and other such abbreviations are part of the language kids often use to circumvent what they see as a parental invasion of privacy.

I will never forget the frantic mother who approached me following my media seminar at a suburban Detroit parish. This mom had planned a weekend getaway with her husband and thought she had prepared things well. Her parents had come over to stay and watch her two children. She had stocked the fridge with all of their favorite foods and had given strict instructions for bedtime and appropriate television viewing. She also placed limits on how much television the children could watch.

However, this mother was no match for her nine-year-old daughter who, unbeknownst to her loving parents and grandparents, was a computer whiz. While mom and dad were away and grandma and grandpa were doing their best babysitting, the little girl was in her room working away on the computer. In one weekend she developed her own website, complete with pictures and personal information, including her name, the name of her school, and her school activities. She was breaking every rule in the Internet safety book. The mom returned home from a relaxing getaway only to find several emotional phone messages from concerned parents whose children told them all about the nine-year-old's "cool web site." Little did they know that there surely were predators who, using their own computer tricks, would find her site and begin to ruminate on the possibilities.

Because of a ripple effect, even those of us fortunate enough not to have directly experienced media-related heartbreak or drama are forced to respond to the influence of the noise in our society. In his 2004 address on World Communications Day, Pope John Paul II warned us about the media's potentially devastating impact on individuals and families:

> Thanks to the unprecedented expansion of the communications market in recent decades, many families throughout the world, even those of quite modest means, now have access in their own homes to immense and varied media resources. ...Yet these same media also have the capacity to do grave harm

> to families by presenting an inadequate or even
> deformed outlook on life, on the family, on religion,
> and on morality.[8]

This book is meant to outline the problem of media noise and its impact on individuals, families, and society. The research is compiled from a variety of sources including research groups, universities, and professional organizations that have been studying the effect of the media for many years. In these pages, though, we go even further by offering practical suggestions on how to silence the noise, which even the U.S Census Bureau concedes continues to get louder and louder. According a report released in December 2006, both adults and teens will spend nearly five months (or about 3,500 hours) surfing the Internet, watching television, listening to the radio, or using other media devices.[9]

With this in mind, be assured that ours is not an easy mission, but we can take comfort in Jesus' promise that "in the world you have tribulation; but be of good cheer, I have overcome the world" (John 16:33).

CHAPTER 1

Am I Nuts, or Is It Bad Out There?

"Christmas is a tree with lights all aglow.
Christmas is a candy cane with fresh and glistening snow."

After reciting those words for my third-grade Christmas play, I was "bitten by the bug," as they say in the broadcast biz. I had discovered my gift for gab at an early age, and from that moment I was on a mission to pursue a career in broadcasting. I pursued it with great focus and met with success early. My high school and college years were filled with stints at campus newspapers and radio stations. Two college internships at major stations in Detroit helped me build up my resume, and I landed my first job at a small southeastern Michigan radio station right after graduating college in 1981. At the rate I was going, I knew I was on the fast track to land a coveted broadcast position on a local network affiliate, and maybe even at the national level.

I was a sponge, soaking up the techniques necessary to advance my career and my agenda, which at the time was simply to make a difference in the community, even if that meant breaking just one big story. Most journalists have similarly altruistic goals—a desire to present the facts, touch hearts, and change minds. Equally enticing, though, is the constant adrenaline rush the news business offers. I loved this aspect of the business. Journalists have an instinctive desire to be the first to cover breaking news. It is exhausting but very gratifying because, after hours of tracking down a story, finding an appealing angle, and giving it identity, there is satisfaction in presenting it to the public. In short, I listened, learned, and jockeyed for position as almost everyone does in this highly competitive profession.

Mastering the art of self-promotion is necessary to thrive in such a fast-paced environment. This often turns the job into a nasty game of one-upmanship. In school, I learned the art of self-promotion and became quite good at it. Since the media is a dog-eat-dog business that devours the thin-skinned, I had to do what it took to survive. The process may not often reflect Christian values, but sometimes principles have to take a backseat to accomplishments, or so I thought. Much success—and also tough times—in a heartless business followed, but I loved everything about being a news anchor and reporter: the rush of a breaking story, the high energy level of the newsroom, and especially the notion that I was providing a valuable public service.

Consumed with my career, I failed to notice that the standards which had been ingrained in me by my faithful parents and through my Catholic education lost their prominence as I forged ahead in my profession. Ego was a key factor, to be sure. In fact, ego can very well be an acronym for Easing God Out, which is exactly what I did. The more success I had, the more my ego grew, and God became smaller in the process. I was so consumed with my own agenda that pretty soon any remnants of my Catholic faith vanished. My selfish obsession with succeeding almost cost me my marriage as well as my soul. I was losing my way, but I didn't realize it. Broadcast standards had been spiraling downward, even faster than society at large. Apathy enabled us to accept the escalating noise in our lives, and the noise prevented us from distinguishing suitable decorum from rubbish. Looking back now, I realize that I was gradually being prepared for a wake-up call from God, but first I had to be open to receiving Him. I had to hit rock bottom.

My moment of revelation was slow to come. It took getting fired from my first major TV news job to start the awakening process. Getting fired (or laid off, whatever one chooses to call it), while common in today's tough economic climate, is still difficult. One might think in the cutthroat business of broadcasting, where anchors and reporters are frequently replaced with someone younger, that the sting is somehow less painful because change is so common. But when your name and face are all over the TV screen every night, it is actually much worse. You are forced to explain repeatedly to people at church, the grocery store, or the mall why you are not on the air any longer, and since you are never given a reason by the news bosses for your departure, it makes the entire situation that much more uncomfortable.

My dismissal, though thoroughly unpleasant, was by far the best thing that ever happened to me. Thanks to Michigan's slow economy, with the exception of some freelance work, I was unemployed and off the air for nearly six months. I had been knocked off my high horse. I was humbled, and it was during this desert time that I was forced to take a good look at myself, my marriage, my profession, and, most importantly, my relationship (or lack thereof) with God. Thanks to a loving husband and his strong faith, I began to get my life back on track. I finally began taking my faith more seriously and prayed for direction as to what God wanted me to do. My Catholic religion, which I had for the most part ignored, was a great comfort and healer to me—especially the Mass and the sacrament of reconciliation. I slowly made my way back into the Church and back onto the airwaves, landing a prestigious reporting job at another local network TV affiliate. Then, a few years later, I was back on radio in a prime-time shift. But that is when I started to notice something was not right. Why, after I had worked for more than two decades in television and radio, had my passion for the industry begun to wane? I had seen some bias in the news business and I'd had my share of run-ins regarding editorial content with coworkers, news directors, and other management types, but such differences were just part of the landscape—part of what kept the newsroom balanced. By the late 1990s, however, I began to realize that the discord that once fueled me had drained me. This was deeply disturbing because I was no quitter, yet I was becoming weary. I tried to convince myself that the early morning hours and subsequent lack of sleep were getting to me, but I think I knew all along this was not the problem. I had landed a well-paying dream job as the morning-drive newswoman on a major Detroit FM station. My profession had taken me from radio to television and back to radio. So why was I miserable?

Something was wrong, and it was not all about me. I knew something was terribly flawed with the business for which I had studied so hard and sacrificed so much time and effort. My professional world seemed to be falling apart around me. Like all journalists, I always strived to be objective. College professors and news directors had always emphasized the importance of getting the whole story and reporting it objectively, yet integrity had begun taking a backseat to news reports that were built around paid commercials rather than on the delivery of helpful information. In 1979, a typical hourly newscast on a music-formatted radio station was five to six minutes long. By 1999, news on music radio, if it existed at all, consisted of a mere thirty seconds of headlines, sports scores, weather, and a "kicker" (i.e., lighthearted story) all wrapped around commercial taglines and finished in two minutes or less. All my years of schooling and paying dues as an intern, and all the long hours I had invested in interviewing, reporting, and capturing video footage, had been whittled down to barely two minutes of fluff over the airwaves. It seemed no one was interested in serious news coverage, just headlines and feature stories on the sex lives of celebrities. I understood the value of entertainment in media, the "lure them in and keep them" mentality, but I also came to realize that rather than serving the public interest, the news industry existed to serve the almighty dollar. In my heart, I knew the weariness I was feeling came from frustration with the job I was beginning to detest and a total disillusionment with the media in general.

The mass media had already gone to hell in a hand basket, and the reality of just how nasty it had become was present for all but the most morally blind to see. "If it bleeds, it leads" was (and remains) the modus operandi in radio, television, and printed news coverage. The shock value of video or pictures from murders, fires, or accident scenes placed those stories ahead of in-depth reports on education and politics. Though one can only rarely refer to a Hollywood movie as prophetic, the state of the media very much resembled *Network*, the 1976 film about TV executives and talent appealing to the lowest common denominator for the sake of ratings. Scenes from the movie constantly ran through my head, and I wasn't alone in my concern over declining standards. Plenty of other burned-out broadcasters lamented the state of the industry. Contacts of mine who served as station managers and program directors complained about "feeling the heat from corporate" to crank up the ratings by sinking lower and lower in the realm of moral decency and journalistic integrity. Reporter friends were equally fed up with their silly and sensational assignments. Any decent coverage on faith issues had long disappeared from the evening news and front pages. Radio programming had been filled with mindless chatter and the oversexed and immature conversation of shock jocks. Prime-time television had become packed with ridiculous game shows, talk shows, and a budding new format called reality TV.

My struggles of the heart were amplified as government and law-enforcement officials issued reports on the connections between media exposure to violence and the rash of school shootings. I was adopting the mind-set that the media was more of a hindrance than a help to society. No one, however, from within the media seemed willing to do anything about it. After all, broadcasting is a very insecure business. Frustration on the part of media professionals usually gives way to fear of being fired. In fact, the joke within the industry is that radio and television stations should install revolving doors to accommodate the constant staff changes. To swim against the tide is to write your own pink slip. Therefore, most (including me) remained silent and just tried to make the best of it.

In 1999, I came close to caving in and was about to convince myself to just go along for the ride for as long as it lasted. Then, a *USA Today* cover story grabbed my attention and made my epiphany complete. I had just delivered my last newscast on a Monday morning and was anxious for noon to roll around so I could head home. That once foreign feeling of wanting to be anywhere but at work was now commonplace. I sat back, sipped my coffee, and picked up the paper. The headline read, "No TV for Children Under Two."[10] The American Academy of Pediatrics (AAP) report that followed was my tipping point. It was also the answer to my prayers.

I wasn't nuts, after all. Things really were bad out there, and now a major professional organization was concerned enough to speak up. The AAP had introduced a new policy calling for its members to discuss the dangers of television viewing with the parents of toddlers. In unusually strong language, the AAP insisted that even mild TV watching affected the attention spans of young children. The AAP also suggested that exposure to violence, sexual content, and unhealthy foods directly influences the attitudes of children toward these issues.[11] The story was my catalyst. I was instantly rejuvenated and motivated. I grabbed my reporter's notebook and began chronicling with vigor. I had a story worth pursuing and a cause in need of a response. I was eager to learn more about media influence on society, and I felt that I was called to do something about the sleaze and sensationalism that permeated my beloved field. I had the experience to find the facts and the determination to find solutions. Deep down, I had always believed that when used properly, the media could be a force for good.

If you want God to laugh, make plans. This old adage pretty much sums up my life. I pursued *my* plans in high school, college, and in the news world, and I ended up nearly divorced, burned out, and disillusioned with the industry I loved. Yet my prayers had been answered. God took away that which was ultimately contributing to my demise and created in me a new heart (Psalm 51) and renewed my mind (Romans 12:2). The message became clear: I was not to leave the problem—the media—but become a part of the solution. I decided to remain in the industry about which I cared so passionately, but on God's terms this time. In 2000, I made that move in earnest by taking a job as a talk-show host on Christian radio station WMUZ-FM. Within months, my desire broadened into establishing a larger media-ministry apostolate. Heeding this call, I now travel North America offering an insider's perspective on the effects of mass media on our culture and families, and I offer suggestions for exacting change. God has blessed the five loaves and two fish I brought to the table by expanding my radio audience in 2006 to national levels. I now reach a potential audience of millions in more than a hundred markets and on EWTN and satellite radio. What God can do with our simple "yes" is truly wonderful.

Is it really bad out there? The short answer is yes. In the seven years since I have embarked on this mission, morality in the media has spiraled downward at a rate much faster than most had anticipated. As we will see in the coming chapters, the media culture is fueling an immorality rarely seen in human history. It is disrupting family life like never before and filling our heads with a constant clamor of noise. As a result, the worship of our good God has become a preeminent casualty in this competition for our hearts, minds, and souls. That said, grassroots movements are popping up in response to the media Goliath, and with a gentle wind blown in the right direction, they will spread like wildfire.

CHAPTER 2

It's No Big Deal

As I stepped down from the podium following my presentation on the media at a 2004 women's retreat in Ottawa, Canada, a woman looking distraught approached me, grabbed my hand, and thanked me for my ministry. "I was led to believe it was no big deal," she began, "until I found out that my son was addicted to Internet pornography and violent video games." She went on to explain that her fourteen-year-old son had just completed intensive therapy for his media addictions. She had never imagined things would get as bad as they did, but as her son spent more and more time on the computer, his life (and that of the entire family) began to spin out of control.

Unfortunately, many of us think, "It's no big deal," and as long as the media moguls are making billions, they will never take a serious look at the poison spewing from their money machines. Phrases like, "It's only a TV show," "It's just a game," or "It's free speech," or "art," or "literature" cause consumers and professionals alike to doubt their own instincts. I would consistently hear these types of responses as I uncovered mounds of evidence showing how deeply we all are affected by the messages we hear, read, or see in the media. At the time, it seemed as though the general population—including the Christian community—did not want to face the truth. Even studies released by credible secular organizations failed to rouse the public's ire or even interest.

If media influence is "no big deal," then why did the American Academy of Pediatrics (AAP) find it necessary to issue a major policy statement regarding the dangers of television viewing among toddlers?[12] Why did they launch Media Matters, a national media education campaign? If it's truly "no big deal," then why did the Federal Trade Commission (FTC) investigate the sale of violent video games to minors following the Columbine shootings?[13] Finally, why do so many universities, professional organizations, faith and family values groups, government agencies, law enforcement, and medical and psychological experts continue to study, research, write, speak, and warn against media influence? It is, in fact, a big deal. The opinions, moral choices, and religious expressions of tens of millions of Americans and hundreds of millions of people worldwide have been profoundly influenced by the media.

According to a 2001 study by the AAP, the connection between media violence and violence in real life "has been substantiated with as much as ten to twenty percent of real-life violence attributed to violence in the media."[14]

A seventeen-year longitudinal study by the Kaiser Family Foundation issued in 2003 found that teens who watched more than one hour of television a day were almost four times as likely to commit aggressive acts in adulthood.[15] After the Columbine shootings, law enforcement discovered that the two gunmen in the school massacre were both hooked on violent video games. As a result, the FTC started to conduct undercover shopping stings using underage teens to see just how many M-rated (i.e., mature) games were being sold to minors.[16] A startling March 2006 American Medical Association (AMA) survey found that media images of college girls partying during spring break might contribute to an increase in reckless behavior, including excessive drinking and premarital sex.[17] How did the noise become so dangerous?

Several factors have contributed to the current sorry state of the mass media: the very real liberal agenda of Hollywood; increased competition from cable TV; the Telecommunications Act of 1996, which led to media consolidation; and the placement of profit before public interest. Add to this recipe a large quantity of consumer apathy, and watch the revenues of stock market-driven media conglomerates grow. So we cannot expect the media giants to pull the reins in on themselves until their bottom line is affected. Time Warner, Sony, Disney, CBS, Viacom, Bertelsmann, Hearst, General Electric, News Corporation, Liberty Media, and Comcast are concerned only about deals that translate to greater revenues. These conglomerates have the support of Hollywood producers, radio and TV management, program and news directors, porn-site operators, video game makers, and anyone else who earns a living through the direct or indirect marketing and distribution of products that compromise the values on which this country was founded. Although they appear to be in denial, the media mega-powers know that it *is* a big deal, and they even occasionally give us a glimpse of their own awareness of their pervasive influence. Such was the case when CBS president Les Moonves candidly stated to a *Washington Post* reporter, "Anyone who thinks the media [have] nothing to do with [youth violence] is an idiot."[18]

By default, the mass media has become our voice, and worse yet, our barometer of standards. How did a once God-fearing society become so penetrable? Again, like frogs in a pot of slowly boiling water, we have been cooking for some time. Research on the matter has led to some eye-opening facts about human nature and the current state of the media beast. The chapters that follow offer a credible analysis of human character and a discussion of the dumbing-down effects of media noise, as well as statistics on the harmful impact of this noise on our culture and real accounts of its negative effect on the lives of individuals.

CHAPTER 3

Are You Strong Enough?

On some level, most of us sense that we simply cannot maintain a steady diet of media saturation without some negative side effects. The obvious harmful result of such indulgence is decreased morality, but few realize its more pernicious effect. Catholic psychologist Dr. Gregory Popcak passed on a discovery that was new to me but a common thought among mystics, saints, and even deep secular thinkers for hundreds, if not thousands, of years. It is a simple truth, but one that has dramatic ramifications for our modern culture. It contends that all significant human development—psychological, intellectual, emotional, and spiritual—comes through reflection. That is, our highest faculty as a human person is our mind. The mind is where we discern, reflect, choose, and finally, decide to act. These factors determine whether we grow, regress, or remain stagnant. In the mind, particularly through the act of reflection, we determine how we will respond to life, to others, and to the wisdom and grace that God provides.

Now, consider the ramifications of rarely (or never) reflecting. What if we were to become so desirous of being entertained, or so accustomed to simply responding to stimuli, that we rarely had a chance to actually think about ourselves and our direction in life? In a sense, we would become less than human. Instead of being proactive we would be merely reactive, and eventually the stimuli would dominate, stunting our growth and jeopardizing our self-identities. We would risk not knowing who we are, why we are here on earth, and where we are headed in both this life and eternity. In short, over-indulgence in noise clouds our thinking, and it is perhaps the most devastating effect of our dominant media culture. It is the reason many of us place more emphasis on the Super Bowl than on our spiritual lives. The noise is so attractive, so intoxicating, and so loud that we drown in the distraction.

Popcak offers fascinating insights on identity and human development. He lists three basic identity types: *immature, functional,* and *strong.* Because identity is the foundation upon which we build and live our lives, forging a strong identity is crucial to progressing intellectually, psychologically, emotionally, and spiritually. The *immature identity* is overly concerned with externals like appearance, material possessions, and friends or associates. Such an identity is typical in adolescents and young adults. The problem with building a life around such fleeting realities is that those realities could easily disappear, causing our identity to disappear along with them.

Those who define themselves by their role in life, such as a career, job title, cause, or status, have a *functional identity.* This is common from young adulthood to about age forty. Although significantly better than an immature identity, the person with a functional identity can have problems if he or she stops developing at this point. In addition, one's functional identity can be instantly lost if the person is fired or discovers that his or her cause is no longer worth fighting. An additional danger of the functional identity is that many at this level think they have "made it" because their role in life is "bigger than themselves." Such a role can be noble and meaningful.

The *strong identity* is determined by life choices, which are based on one's core values and beliefs. Those with strong identities actively live in pursuit of goodness, truth, prudence, faith, hope, love, etc., and they can quickly spot counterfeits. A strong identity is often the result of some sort of conversion to faith or other life-altering experience, and is capable of weathering storms. A person with a strong identity is countercultural, or as St. Paul tells us, a "new creation" (see 2 Corinthians 5:17). A strong identity is not easily lost to sudden weight gain, hair loss, or stock market drop. The mere fact that you are reading this book is likely evidence of your strong character. You have already determined that something is amiss in our culture and you want to do something about it. The problem we are facing as a media- and technology-dominated culture is that such a culture inherently works against the forging of strong identities. The person with a weak identity—one built on superficial things—loves the glitz and glamour of the "fabulous life" seen in the media. He allows the culture to dictate how he acts or thinks, and likely gravitates toward shows that merely entertain while subtly pushing a superficial lifestyle. The body image woes of women at this level will be fueled by the ultra-thin girls on *America's Next Top Model*, and their hearts might be temporarily placated by the promise offered by plastic surgeons on *Dr. 90210*. Some may shell out thousands of dollars to look better, but most will live their lives believing their appearance is flawed.

The same is also true, albeit a little less so, for those with functional identities. Such people will likely gravitate toward shows like *Survivor* or *The Apprentice*. They will fantasize about using their cunning to win temporal accomplishments, resulting in a more powerful and glamorous life. Many will have moments of nobility—thinking about what they could do for others with such power and success—but most will simply desire to indulge more in that which is fleeting.

Surely, the person with a strong identity faces challenges as well. Such a person, though driven by core values and beliefs, is still a child of the human race; he has a wounded nature. Should he slip into over-indulgence of the dominant media culture, he may grow weaker in his conviction, or simply not allow enough time for reflection, which is where we grow. The media culture is the enemy of those very disciplines that usually result in reflection, contemplation, and growth.

The late Catholic philosopher Dr. William Marra once quipped, "There are so many television channels out there now that if a person so desired he could never have another original thought in his life." An exaggeration, perhaps, but his point is valid. Blessed Teresa of Calcutta (known to most as Mother Teresa) echoed these thoughts when she said, "We need to find God, and he cannot be found in noise and restlessness. God is the friend of silence. See how nature—trees, flowers, grass—grows in silence; see the stars, the moon and the sun, how they move in silence. …We need silence to be able to touch souls."[19] Even secular thinkers also came to the conclusion that distraction was the enemy of human development. One of America's founding fathers, Thomas Paine, wrote, "The real man smiles in trouble, gathers strength from distress, and grows brave by reflection."[20] And it was Socrates who gave us perhaps the most famous gem of all, "The unexamined life is not worth living."[21]

As parents, we have all lamented when our kids have wasted away a beautiful sunny day watching television or playing their XBoxes for hours on end. We want our children to have it all, but we intuitively know that such distractions are often harmful to their maturation. We know our kids are called to more than just being proficient at *Super Mario Brothers*. We are all called to greatness; we are called to be saints. We are called to live lives worthy of the calling of Christ (see Ephesians 4:1). It is likely, though, that the only way we can do this is by breaking the death grip that the noise of the culture and the business of life have on us. It is in stillness that we will best come to know God and our very selves. As Christians, we were given the virtues of faith, hope, charity, wisdom, understanding, fortitude, and much more in baptism, but they need to be exercised. They need to be nurtured. In order to reflect on these truths or to hear God's voice, we must turn down the world's volume. It is difficult to do this with a remote in our hands, flipping through channels.

CHAPTER 4

The Creation of the Self-Absorbed Blob

His name is Taylor, but his parents refer to him as "caveman" because he spends just about every waking minute behind closed doors playing video games. This unmotivated sixteen-year-old comes out of his room every now and then to eat, but antsiness prevents him from hanging out at the dinner table with mom and dad very long; his video games beckon him like a homing beacon.

Meet eleven-year-old Cole, who gets home from school at about two o'clock in the afternoon, goes up to his room, plops himself on his bed, and grabs the remote. He spends several hours alone glued to the television watching MTV and *Dukes of Hazzard* reruns.

Stephen, forty-nine, has once again eaten dinner late and alone. His family no longer waits for him to wrap up business on his cell phone or log off his e-mail. Stephen's fourteen-year-old son has been upstairs in his bedroom for hours logged onto MySpace.com. His daughter, Bronte, has already commandeered his laptop so she can do her homework while chatting on her cell phone. The family may be home together, but they are connected to their electronics rather than to each other. Taylor, Cole, and Stephen are real people from real American families, who by their own admissions are absolutely absorbed in the world of the wired (and the world of the wireless, for that matter). Taylor and Cole were featured in a front-page *USA Today* article on media usage.[22] Stephen and his two children were part of a *Time* cover story on the same topic.[23] Stephen's family had been taking part in a four-year study of modern family life conducted by UCLA's Center on Everyday Lives of Families. Despite their individual virtues, rampant media dependence has molded each into a kind of self-absorbed blob. As harsh as that sounds, it is the sad truth. We are literally being entertained to death. The noise inhibits our ability to grow, thus creating a cadre of consumers.

Contrary to self-donation (i.e., giving of ourselves to others), self-absorption results when we place primary focus on sating self, usually to the exclusion of others. Few would deny that beyond feeling compelled to respond to noble charitable outreach efforts like those that followed Hurricane Katrina in 2005 or the devastating tsunami that hit Southeast Asia in 2004, we are a radically self-absorbed society. The dominance of the media and the endless lineup of gadgets fuel this reality. The situation is so bad that *Time* reporters felt compelled to point out the obvious in their list of suggested family activities. They advise parents to "enjoy your children" and to do "mundane, non-technological things: wash the car together, play Ping-Pong together, debate politics, and take [children] out for ice cream."[24]

The inherent need to upgrade to the latest and greatest electronic device only perpetuates a vicious cycle of self-absorption—a cycle that is preyed upon by advertisers and played out in every form of entertainment. In short, the media appeals to our learned instinct to "keep up with the Joneses." We have to have the fastest computer, the newest Blackberry, the sleekest flat-screen TV, portable GPS navigation, as well as household appliances that rival those on *The Jetsons*. As a result, we are convinced that we simply cannot be happy without these gadgets. According to psychologists, the best way to avoid entrapment in the self-absorption cycle is to reduce exposure to the media. Included in *Time*'s list of solutions is the recommendation to eat dinner together as a family. Family dinners were nowhere to be found in the daily routines of the folks in the aforementioned study groups. A 2005 Columbia University survey found that teenagers who ate dinner with their families at least five times per week were more likely to get better grades and avoid substance-abuse problems than those who did not participate regularly in family meals.[25]

Faced with the troubles that plague our society, why do we continue to indulge? Perhaps we are attempting to fill a deep void, one that is temporarily filled with godlike entertainment and gadgetry. There is no doubt that we live in a marvelously advanced age. It is truly mind-blowing that we can fit a thousand songs on a device the size of a cigarette lighter. Likewise, it is extraordinarily entertaining to watch the magic of Hollywood's technicians and artists dazzle the screen with special effects. Ultimately, we all know that these are false gods, and false gods do not satisfy. There are so many of them, however, that we could spend our entire lives jumping from one to the next, allowing for little or no down time in between. Thus is our cultural dilemma. The great American spirit of invention, problem solving, and artistic expression is terrific, but if we do not temper our intake of these creations, they will consume us. In many ways, they already have. Contentious Catholics and other people of good will are taking steps to stem the tide. The question that remains is whether the media monster has infected the world beyond repair. My instinctive response is yes, but I know that with Christ, there is always hope. While there have been and will continue to be casualties in our war against the deafening noise of the media, we must not give in to discouragement and surrender. The stakes are too high.

CHAPTER 5

The Loss of Reason

One morning in the spring of 2006, I was giving my Catholic radio listeners my two cents as to why any and every God-fearing person on the planet should avoid *The Da Vinci Code* like the plague and not give their hard-earned money to Dan Brown, Tom Hanks, Ron Howard, Sony, or anyone else associated with such blasphemy. I pointed out that while the book and the film claimed to be a fictional story built on facts, the alleged "facts" about the Scriptures and Church history were nowhere to be found in either the novel or the movie. Catholic writer and historian Sandra Miesel said it best when she remarked, "The only thing Dan Brown seemed to get right was that Paris is in France and London is in England."[26] Nearly everything else in *The Da Vinci Code* is sheer nonsense. This fact didn't stop Sony from inviting moviegoers to "seek the truth" and shell out out nine dollars each to see the movie, generating more than $600 million in ticket sales and offending countless Christians in the process. I did whatever I could to give my listeners the ammunition I thought they would need to stand up against the lies, distortions, and fabrications in Brown's blatantly anti-Catholic story, but such efforts were no match for the financial power of Sony and Doubleday, the book's publisher.

Despite my best efforts and sincerest pleas to educate and inform Catholics and other Christians as to why they should stay away from *The Da Vinci Code,* that morning I realized I still had a lot of work to do. One of my regular listeners called to say she was going to see the movie because "we should be open to opinions about our faith so we can learn more." After I picked my jaw up from the floor, I told her that Brown's "opinion" of Christianity in general and the Catholic Church in particular was not based in reality. He either intentionally pulled the wool over millions of readers' eyes or would have to go down in history as one of the worst researchers the world has known. To my horror she responded, "That just can't be. After all, the media would never print or say anything that wasn't true."

Such a statement, from a Catholic radio listener no less, reveals another casualty in the cultural battle fueled by our addiction to media, entertainment, and gadgetry: the loss of reason. Millions of people take what the media says as gospel. They seem eager to believe high-school teacher Dan Brown over Pope Benedict XVI—despite the fact that Brown has no credentials as an historian, theologian, or art critic, while Benedict XVI is widely acknowledged as a scholar of the highest degree, as well as being the successor of St. Peter and the Vicar of Christ.

A "loss of reason" occurs when we allow feelings, emotions, or plain old laziness to trump the sometimes demanding task of thinking logically. When we no longer use our reason, we make our choices based on sentimentality at the expense of proven or revealed truths. Due in no small part to our addiction to entertainment, many of us have allowed our highest natural gift, our intellect, to remain in idle mode as important issues in the world come across our desks, are discussed in our dinner conversations, are taught in our high-school classrooms and college lecture halls, or most often, are brought to us through the media. The gift of a well-formed intellect allows us to think critically about the issues and events that confront us on a daily basis. Without using our intellects, we are open to being manipulated by the cultural spin doctors, media pundits, and Hollywood elite. Thus, many of us are turning to the *New York Times* and even *Jerry Springer* and the *National Enquirer* for "truth" instead of picking up the Bible, the *Catechism*, or engaging in articulate dialogue. The intoxicating allure of entertainment found in the media has generated potentially millions of consumers who are simply not thinking. We seem to be merely responding, usually to the position that requires the least amount of thought.

The radio listener mentioned earlier is a cradle Catholic who earnestly practices her faith. She has gone to Mass her entire life. However, her understanding of the faith, or lack thereof, was no match for today's massive media marketing machine. As a result, she was either unable or unwilling to think for herself. Evidently, neither were millions of others in America and around the world who, despite countless bad reviews of the film, packed theatres the weekend of May 19, 2006 to see *The Da Vinci Code*. Is it any surprise that a 2005 National Geographic survey found that one-third of Canadians who read the *The Da Vinci Code* actually believe Dan Brown's claims that Jesus' descendants are alive and well, and living happily ever after in Europe? In an interview with United Press International, Vanessa Case, vice president of programming for the National Geographic Channel and Life Network, said readers felt like they were being let in on "an explosive historical secret. It is obvious that *The Da Vinci Code* has had a huge impact on Canadians and their beliefs," she added.[27] This should not surprise us. Our lives are so busy with work, kids, school activities, and watching television that the convenience of letting the media think for us has become a natural occurrence. My listener is just one example of the loss of reason that engulfs the public at large.

Another study dramatizes the extent to which our judgment is clouded. A 2006 survey conducted by researchers in Washington, D.C. found that one out of three *American Idol* viewers believe that voting for their favorite contestant is just as important as voting for the

President of the United States.[28] The priorities of young Americans—as well as their abysmal lack of geographical knowledge—were revealed in yet another study, which found that despite the endless news coverage of the war in Iraq, sixty-three percent could not find Iraq on a map of the Middle East.[29] Sound like an episode of *Ripley's Believe It or Not?* It gets better. Only half of those questioned could find New York State on a map of the United States. In addition, one-third of the respondents were unable to find Louisiana, despite the extensive news coverage of the Gulf Coast following Hurricane Katrina.[30]

The noise in our society is a major contributing factor to generations of children with little or no attention span. A major piece on education in *USA Today* quoted psychologists as saying that it is becoming increasingly difficult to keep kids' attention because they need constant entertainment.[31] The study points out the skyrocketing diagnoses of attention-deficit hyperactivity disorder, or ADHD. Researchers lay much of the blame on the fast-paced media. Our fifty-year diet of television, and the more recent indulgence by youth in video games, has adversely affected our capacity for sustained thinking. Modern advertising techniques substantiate this phenomenon by the fact that there are an increasing number of fifteen-second commercials. Historically, television commercials ran thirty or sixty seconds long.

Considering the fact that our ability to reason is by far the most important attribute for success in life, we must think about the ramifications of indulging our children's desires for media entertainment. As individuals and as a culture, we pay a dear price for apathy, and we will continue to pay that price unless we stem this tide. The problem can only worsen as the number of media outlets and electronic entertainment options multiply, and new generations are raised without ever being introduced to alternatives to the noise. Most importantly, not only is our children's and our own temporal success at stake but also our very souls. An idle mind is indeed the devil's playground, and it is time for us to stand up to that bully in the playground.

CHAPTER 6

Is It Soup Yet?

It's five o'clock. Do you know where your family is? Why is something as simple as eating dinner together such a challenge for most families and a totally foreign concept for others? Joseph Califano Jr. laments, "If I could wave a magic wand to make a dent in the substance abuse problem, I would make sure that every child in America had dinner with his or her parents at least five times a week. There is no more important thing a parent can do. Parental engagement in children's lives is the key to ridding our nation of the scourge of substance abuse." Califano chairs the National Center on Addiction and Substance Abuse, which, ironically, is known by the acronym CASA (Spanish for *house*). He made the previous statement after CASA released its 2005 study *The Importance of Family Dinners II*.[32] Research shows that less than half of U.S. families eat together on a regular basis, and when the family does sit down, distractions often prevail. If the breakdown of society is a reflection of the breakdown of family, then what are we doing to fortify the family unit?

Granted, media gadgetry cannot shoulder the entire blame. Over the years many families have become accustomed to dinner with the television on. Another distraction is the newspaper. I have a friend who races to get dinner on the table just so the tabletop will be covered before her husband enters the kitchen. She wants to leave him no room to lay the mail or the newspaper. Simply asking him to leave his reading material off the table while the family is eating had only sparked arguments in the past.

Another challenge to a quality dinnertime is the eat-and-run participants, usually children. I have heard from parents who regrettably allow their kids to leave the table immediately upon woofing down their food because they are too battle weary to argue with their kids. Another mom joked with me about getting old when she didn't notice until halfway through dinner that her teenage son was wearing ear buds (tiny headsets that fit inside the ear and connect to an iPod or MP3 player). She thought he was unusually well-behaved that particular night because he wasn't taunting his younger sister. Instead, he was listening to music on his iPod. Each of these examples can easily be fixed with a set of family rules, but we are often so drained by the daily demands of life that even when rules are established, consequences for failing to comply are not implemented. The result is a lack of cooperation. Now, combine those various distractions with media messages that contradict traditional family values and the net result is often a fractured family or immoral lifestyles.

Children are spending so much time watching television or chatting online that today's youth have been labeled "Generation-M," which stands for media or multitasking. Worse than the mere distractions are the types of messages to which Generation-M is exposed. Kids are no longer watching family shows like *Leave it to Beaver, The Waltons,* or *Little House on the Prairie.* According to the Nielsen ratings, the most popular show among nine to twelve-year-old girls in 2005 was ABC's *Desperate Housewives.*[33] We certainly do not need a government-sponsored study to show us how a steady diet, or even one serving, of deception, adultery, and fornication is bad for children. Whether we like it or not, the women of Wisteria Lane are huge role models for both younger and older women. Imagine the long-term ramifications. Imagine the future makeup of the PTA, Women's Auxiliary, or state and federal congressional houses. Perhaps the lowering of moral standards fueled by a steady diet of soap operas, sitcoms, and lewd lyrics explains why so many women were so forgiving of the smooth-talking Bill Clinton, despite the fact that he broke his marital vows when he preyed on a young female intern.

Desperate Housewives is but one example of the many shows spewing anti-family messages on network television. A quick visit to the Parent Television Council website (www. parentstv.org) reveals media moral failings that would cause some salty sailors to blush. Worse yet, network executives use words such as "family" or "dad" or "American" or "home" in the names of many of the programs to convince viewers that the shows are family-friendly. Consider *The Family Guy* or *American Dad* or *The War at Home.* These shows are filled with sexual content, outright nudity, crude and foul language, and negative portrayals of anyone who is remotely conservative or, heaven forbid, a Christian. Also noted in recent decades is the consistent portrayal of buffoon-like fathers. Gone are the days of responsible TV dads like Ward Cleaver and Ozzie Nelson. Since the sexual revolution of the 1960s, America has been fathered by *Bewitched*'s bumbling Darrin Stevens, *All in the Family*'s bigoted Archie Bunker, *Married with Children*'s lustful Al Bundy, and *The Simpsons'* doltish Homer Simpson. Over the past three decades or so, the model TV dad has been portrayed as an overweight, underachieving, sexually-obsessed racist.

A television program, however, does not have to build its plot around a family in order for it to contribute to the breakdown of the family. Other popular shows, whether on cable or broadcast television, contain so much sex, violence, and crime that behavior which was once considered unacceptable, immoral, or even illegal is now portrayed as normal and commonplace. Wife-swapping, sex parties, and mother-son incest were just a few of the things viewers have been treated to on popular shows such as CBS' *CSI: Crime Scene Investigation.* The result is that moms and dads struggling to raise their children in faith-filled homes are portrayed as, and made to feel, abnormal. "If it *feels* good, it *is* good" is the common message being streamed from the likes of TV, music, movies, and various Internet sites. The message is aimed at each of us: children, teens, young adults, and older adults. Advertisers know how to appeal to all demographics. Whether it is "Grabbing the gusto" or "doing the Dew," the purpose is to appeal to our self-centered nature. Directly or indirectly, the media mantra advises us to set aside principles that might inhibit our pursuit of self. Is it any wonder that we see a continuing breakdown of the family? The divorce rate in the United States is still extremely high, with close to fifty percent of first marriages expected to end in divorce and single-parent households are on the rise.[34] It is no wonder that this "all about me" approach has led to a breakdown of morality and ultimately a breakdown of the family.

CHAPTER 7

The Inmates are Running the Asylum

S andra was a young mother struggling with disciplining her daughter. She called my talk show one day to speak with my guest, a Christian counselor who was promoting an upcoming seminar on discipline. Among other things, my guest was going to teach parents how to say no to their children. A generation or two ago, such a seminar would have been found only in the psychology labs of liberal universities. Today, parents are ready to shell out money to relearn their God-given rights, and quite frankly, their responsibilities. Sandra explained how her daughter was rebellious and basically did what she wanted in the home. Mom and daughter fought about everything, from what the child watched on television to what time she went to bed and wore to school. Sandra claimed she had a hard time saying no, and instead tried to reason with and explain herself to her daughter. This modern technique only led to more fighting. I felt sorry for Sandra. She sounded totally frustrated and emotionally exhausted. I envisioned a brazen, "hell on wheels" fifteen- or sixteen-year-old storming in and out of her bedroom and driving her parents nuts. Imagine my surprise after learning the age of the unruly little girl. Very matter-of-factly, Sandra stated that her daughter was eight-years-old. I was dumbfounded! I couldn't believe the home was being run ragged by an eight-year-old, and her parents were letting it happen. Here I was feeling sorry for the listener and thinking an out-of-control teen was showing no respect to the woman who bore and nursed her, when all along, little Pippy was probably still playing with Barbie dolls. My reaction nearly panicked my studio guest.

"Eight years old!" I said. "For crying out loud, you're her mother and she is just a child. Get some backbone and set some boundaries. This is not brain surgery." My Italian temper was in overdrive. My guest looked at me rather nervously, understanding my frustration but trying to signal to me that my outbursts might not have been the best course of action in our mutual effort to help, but I couldn't control my outrage. Just a few seconds later, bearing in mind that a large portion of America was listening, I actually started laughing. Again, I couldn't help it. In an instant, the thought of my tough loving, East Coast Italian mother came to mind. She put up with none of my muscle- (or rather *vocal-*) flexing shenanigans. I tried more than once to exert my agenda, but most times I would be quickly corrected. Afterwards, I knew my boundaries. My dad was a bit of a softie, but he did insist that we respect our mother. My mom didn't have to raise her hands or even her voice. All she had to do was raise her eyebrows and look at my two sisters and me in that certain "I'm going to dismember you" way, and we knew the score. "No" meant "no," not "maybe" and not "if you wouldn't mind, deary." There were rules; if we broke them, we suffered the consequences.

I will never forget one grocery-shopping incident with my mom. Just like most pre-teen girls in the 1970s, I had a crush on heartthrob Bobby Sherman of the popular ABC show *Here Come the Brides*. He was a major TV star and the "it" guy of the teen magazines. One year Bobby signed a deal with Post Raisin Bran. The company included his likeness and one of his hit songs on the cereal box. As we strolled down the cereal aisle, I spotted my favorite celeb on the box and also discovered that a real 45-rpm record was attached. I had never eaten Post Raisin Bran but decided to sneak a box into our cart when mom wasn't looking. I had no intention of eating the stuff. I just figured I would sneak it into the house somehow, throw the cereal away, and keep the box. It was a solid plan until my sharp mother, who I still believe really does have eyes on the back of her head, saw the cereal box rolling down the conveyor belt in the checkout line. Oh, if looks could kill, I would have been terminated at age twelve. The story is so fresh in my mind because my saintly mother made sure I ate every last flake of Raisin Bran before she confiscated my prized box. My parents were raised during the Depression. They frequently told us what it was like to go hungry on occasion and that wasting food was a sin. Mom not only made me eat all the cereal, which I detest to this day, but she also let me have it for trying to get away with something to which I knew she would not have agreed. To further torture this die-hard Sherman fan, mother denied me all *Here Come the Brides* viewing privileges for an entire month. I can laugh about the story now, but at the time it taught me a valuable lesson and put me right in my place.

Why do baby boomers and Gen-Xers have such a difficult time saying no to their children? From my radio audience to the people I meet on the speaking circuit, I constantly hear the same willy-nilly sentiments. It seems as though no one remembers the concept of tough love. As parents, grandparents, aunts, uncles, and guardians of these precious gifts from God, are we so insecure that we fear offending or turning off our children? Or, is it simply a matter of taking the path of least resistance? Is it possible to earn the respect of our children by purchasing all the latest gadgetry for them? We all know families who have media centers that rival the sales displays at Best Buy and Circuit City. Let's face it; children are always going to try to get whatever they can from mom and dad. If we grant all their wishes, though, we should not be surprised when they develop addictions to material things, especially electronic devices. Why would the typically rebellious pre-teen or teenager want to "hang" with mom and dad when he or she has a television, video game console, stereo, and computer in his or her own bedroom? After all, these items entertain without demanding any emotional connection or commitment.

By satisfying our desire to provide children with the luxuries that we didn't have, we are creating a generation of media addicts. In the process, the lure of secular self-gratifying messages all too often pulls them away from God and their family. Parents have expressed to me a concern that they may be damaging their children's psyche by not providing for them all the creature comforts their friends have. What they fail to realize is that by succumbing to the desire to over-provide, parents unwittingly teach their children a "keeping up with the Joneses" mentality. Some moms and dads tell me that they give these material items to their children because they would be hypocrites otherwise. Parents feel guilty saying no to certain influences because of the questionable things they might have done growing up. We often do not recognize, though, that by providing the vehicle for indiscretion, we are subtly condoning questionable behavior. The difference between sneaking a peek at *Playboy* magazine in 1970 and sneaking a peek at porn on the Internet today is that in 1970, most moms and dads were not buying *Playboy* for their boys. In 1970, if mom found a *Playboy* magazine under Johnny's bed, she would tear it to shreds and take away his allowance so that he couldn't buy another one. Parenting today is tougher because, while the Internet is a wonderful tool for learning, it is difficult to monitor our children's activities on-line. (One simple, though not entirely foolproof, solution is to keep the computer in a spot central to the entire family, like the den or rec room. The same can be done with the television and video games.)

Saying no and sticking to it takes resolve. Contrary to popular belief, it is generally easier to say no than to give kids what they want. Many parents will find that they have more power than they realize. After some initial conflict, children will eventually come to respect their parent's no and simply move on. Restricting media usage and issuing strict guidelines on what children are allowed to view, buy, listen to, or do online requires a serious commitment. It also requires teaching children at a young age how to keep themselves occupied. This is also easier than most think. I have a friend who, from the time her children were toddlers, strictly limited their time with electronic devices. She told me that even when she was too busy to play with them, they would occupy themselves playing make-believe or reading. Despite initially complaining when the plug was pulled on their electronics, her children used their imaginations to make up games. Her four children rarely gravitated toward board games, causing my friend to wonder why she ever made the investment. However, her story becomes more encouraging. She noticed that when playing with their electronic games, the house was quiet because there wasn't much interaction between the children. When electronic devices were removed from the equation, her children played together. She says they fought a good bit, too, and although the screaming and yelling would wear on her nerves, she had always thought that it was a natural part of growing and maturing. "How are they going to learn to interact with the outside world if they don't learn how to compromise and get along with their own siblings?" she asked rhetorically. She said that she intervened in her children's disagreements only when absolutely necessary. Now, with two teenagers, one pre-teen, and an eight-year-old, she notices that usually one in the bunch will step up to the role of diplomat to settle arguments before appealing to mom. Granted, family dynamics vary from household to household, but with firm resolve on the part of parents, it is entirely possible to duplicate my friend's scenario.

Parents often feel obligated to fill their children's days with activity and entertainment, but when they place the responsibility on their children to come up with their own activities, they empower them. Such authority helps them gain their independence and grow. The effort requires parents to be prepared with well-thought-out reasons for their decisions, and to stick to those decisions. It means telling our children that other parents are wrong for allowing their kids to watch or listen to certain things. While this may seem difficult at times, it must be done. God has given parents the grace and authority to make these decisions. Parents just need to have the guts to do it.

Last year, a woman attending one of my presentations told me about an interesting conversation she had with another mom she had met at her son's baseball game. The two were talking about the vulgar and violent language in rap music. This woman tried to explain to the other mom that she simply does not allow that kind of music in her home. She also explained how she goes to the store with her children to make sure that they are making wholesome entertainment choices. They check music and movie labels for ratings, and if the material is not suitable, they do not buy it. As a family they also talk about why such music is not acceptable in their home. This woman told me the other mom looked astonished, saying that she could never carry out such an approach because it would require too much follow-up. If we fail to follow-up now, though, we will pay a hefty price later. In many ways, we are already paying. Study after study shows how the media impacts all of us, especially our children. In his 2004 World Communications Day message, Pope John Paul II advised parents to take their responsibilities more seriously when it comes to controlling media outlets in the home. In short, we need to stop letting the kids run the show.

> Parents need to regulate the use of the media in the home. This would include planning and scheduling media usage, strictly limiting the time children devote to the media, making entertainment a family experience, putting some media entirely off limits

and periodically excluding all of them for the sake of other family activities.[35]

The Holy Father's directives may appear to be yet another daunting task in our already busy lives, but take heart: monitoring the media is not all that complicated. Actually, it is relatively easy to begin incorporating prudent media habits into life's daily routine. In the chapters that follow, we will examine each major communications medium to summarize the crippling cultural effects of each on our families. Each chapter closes with a list of ten action steps that will assist in the effort to take control of the media within the family, and eventually, in society. The plan begins with a simple decision to say no to ourselves, our families, and to the media moguls who beam garbage into our lives. This is not child's play; it is a very serious matter.

CHAPTER 8

Television:
A Vast Wasteland

Circa 1973, a chubby seventh-grade Catholic schoolgirl from suburban Detroit, who was tired of being teased about her weight, turned to her mother for help. The young girl wanted to be thin like the teenage girls she saw on all her favorite TV programs and in magazine ads. Her mother agreed to enlist the help of the family pediatrician. Neither the youngster, nor her mother, nor the doctor could foresee that the girl's aspiration would become an uncontrollable obsession. After just a few months of supervised dieting, the girl lost nearly fifteen pounds. She looked and felt better than she ever had before. Though she was finally able to fit into more stylish clothing, she still wasn't completely satisfied. She wasn't as thin as the actress she most admired, Susan Dey of *The Partridge Family*. Like most girls in the early 1970s, this seventh grader had a crush on the show's star, David Cassidy, but she also idolized his razor-thin TV sister, Dey. In an effort to become like Dey, the girl continued dieting beyond the doctor's treatment. She also became adept at avoiding food altogether. Within a matter of months, the once healthy girl starved herself down to

57

eighty-nine pounds and required hospitalization. She was suffering from a newly-diagnosed eating disorder known as anorexia nervosa.

The young girl described above was me. The crisis of my youth, my eating disorder, is another reason I take the topic of media influence so seriously. The media can have a damaging impact on how we view ourselves. If one sitcom can send a young girl over the edge, imagine the collective impact today of two hundred cable channels churning out harmful messages. A relatively innocuous sitcom like *The Partridge Family* is in another moral universe from those of today. Television airwaves are currently dominated by sexually-charged (and increasingly explicit) programs, music videos, and commercials featuring scantily clad, super-skinny supermodels, as well as music videos, dramas, and animated adult comedies featuring vulgar language and violence. A dizzying number of reality shows provide us glimpses into the twisted and sad lives of individuals seeking their fifteen minutes of fame. From the pathetic lifestyle of a drunken Anna Nicole Smith to the depraved exploits of rapper Flavor Flav and his wannabe bimbos, reality shows are pulling television to new lows. The devastating impact such shows collectively have on the minds and souls of our youth is truly incalculable—and downright frightening.

Let's revisit my TV-influenced eating disorder, anorexia nervosa. This psychological illness almost exclusively affects teenage girls and young women, and is marked by faulty eating patterns, malnutrition, and excessive weight loss. Little was known about anorexia in the 1970s, so most of my treatment centered on nutrition and physical recovery. Fortunately, I received a lot of love and attention from my parents because I did not receive psychological counseling. Ironically, Susan Dey has since revealed that she also suffered from an eating disorder during her stint on *The Partridge Family* and as a *Seventeen* magazine covergirl.[36] According to the Anorexia Nervosa and Related Eating Disorders organization (ANRED), more than half of teenage girls are on diets or think they should be.[37] On average, girls begin dieting at age eight, and eighty-one percent of ten-year-old girls in the United States admit they fear becoming fat. A national eating-disorder treatment center reported last year that sixty-three percent of elementary school teachers are concerned about eating disorders in their classroom.[38] From where do these girls get such a poor self-image? Since my diagnosis, psychologists and physicians have come a long way in identifying and treating eating disorders. There are excellent medical facilities around the country that address anorexia and its ugly sister, bulimia, which is characterized by binge eating followed by self-induced vomiting. Even the most experienced medical and mental health professionals, however, face an uphill battle given the massive marketing efforts aimed at girls of all ages. Self-esteem issues and eating disorders represent just a fraction of the problems that stem from media influence, especially television.

Paradoxically, in light of the increased presence of anorexia and bulimia, research also points to media influence as a contributing factor in the increase of obesity in our society. Lack of exercise, combined with constant pressure from the media to indulge, has resulted in an epidemic of both adult and youth obesity among Americans.[39] Compared to their counterparts of fifty years ago, more adults in our technologically-advanced society are able to make a living using their brains as opposed to their brawn. In addition, we are generally better able than our parents or grandparents to afford to eat out, and we do so with increasing frequency. Given the intensity of competition, restaurants are forced to advertise in order to attract consumers. So we do less physical work and have more resources through which advertisers can seduce us to indulge in food and other primal pleasures. Before we address the spiritual ramifications of such indulgence, let's take a look at the physical consequences. A report from the Institute of Medicine and the Committee of Obesity in Children and Youth declared:

> The 21st century began with the new development of an epidemic of childhood obesity. ...The epidemic is affecting boys and girls of all ages across the fifty states, from all socioeconomic strata and ethnic groups—though it disproportionately affects African Americans, Hispanics, and American Indians.[40]

With the exception of sleeping, children spend more time in front of television and electronic screens than they do on any other activity, according to a 1999 report by the Annenberg Public Policy Center.[41] In a joint 2001 study conducted by Johns Hopkins, the National Cancer Institute, and the Centers for Disease Control, researchers found that incidents of obesity were highest among children who watched more than four hours of television per day.[42] A more recent study published in the *International Journal of Obesity* revealed that more than sixty percent of obesity cases can be linked to excess TV viewing.[43] Some lawmakers are so concerned about the childhood epidemic that they are pushing for laws, or have already helped pass laws, to limit or ban the sale of junk food and soft drinks in schools. Media activist organization Commercial Alert lays much of the blame on specific media outlets, including the in-school Channel One. Commercial Alert points out that various in-school television marketing programs run daily ads for products such as Twinkies, Pepsi, Mountain Dew, and various candy bars. The dilemma many schools face is whether they should accept such educational channels free of charge in exchange for airing the supplier's commercials or ban them from their classrooms altogether.

So who is to blame for the vicious cycle? Legal attempts on the part of individuals to hold fast-food restaurants liable for their obesity have been unsuccessful thus far. (Interestingly, though, some local governments—including

New York City—have recently banned the use of transfats by restaurants in their jurisdictions.) It does not seem feasible for the federal government to enact a ban on television food advertising similar to the ban on cigarette advertising passed by Congress in 1970. For the government to seek to eliminate all advertising which has a harmful effect on society is certainly a slippery slope. Such bans could jeopardize the very existence of "free" television and have a deleterious effect on our economy. Ultimately, then, it falls to us as individuals to take responsibility for over-indulging and to monitor the effect such advertising has on ourselves and our children.

Of even greater concern than television's role in promoting eating disorders is the amount of violence that emanates from it and permeates our society. According to *Dying to Entertain,* a Parents Television Council (PTC) report on TV violence issued in January 2007, we should probably forget about the so-called "Family Hour" (8 p.m. to 9 p.m.), once a hallmark of network television, ever returning. Violent acts on television have increased dramatically over the past eight years in every time slot: forty-five percent from 8 p.m. to 9 p.m., ninety-two percent from 9 p.m. to 10 p.m., and 167 percent from 10 p.m. to 11 p.m.[44] In addition, the portrayals of violence are increasingly graphic and explicit. According to PTC president Tim Winters, this disturbing state of affairs is still not enough of a wake-up call for some parents.

Television violence has become a paradox of sorts. Medical and social science have proven conclusively that children are adversely affected by exposure to it—yet millions of parents think nothing of letting their children watch *C.S.I.* or other, equally violent programs. Prominent leaders in the entertainment industry publicly decry violent entertainment – but then continue to produce and distribute it.[45]

Earlier studies indicate that, by the time a child graduates from high school, he or she will have witnessed more than 200,000 violent acts on television, including 16,000 simulated murders.[46] According to the American Academy of Pediatrics (AAP), violence seen in the media may lead not only to aggressive behavior but also to anti-social behavior.[47] Even the very liberal, self-identified atheist Ted Turner, founder of CNN and TBS, is concerned: "Television is the single most significant factor contributing to violence in America."[48] (Rather ironic, given the contribution his networks have made to it.) Violence is the number one concern of social scientists, law-enforcement officials, and advocacy groups. Media violence desensitizes viewers to real violence and increases perceptions that we live in a mean and dangerous world. Perhaps this is why many young people think nothing of taking another's life over something as trivial as a sports team jacket or a pair of sneakers. This mentality might explain why an increasing number of domestic disputes end in murder. It might also explain why many favor convenience over the life of an unborn child or a terminally-ill person, as in abortion and euthanasia.

A common mistake among parents is to allow children to only view "children's programs." The PTC addresses such programming in a report, titled *Wolves in Sheep's Clothing: A Content Analysis of Children's Television*, which found that "there is more violence on children's entertainment programming than on adult oriented TV."[49] Following the release of that study, Brent Bozell, the former president of the PTC, strongly warned parents to beware of that which appears child-friendly:

> While a lot of entertainment programming for children is perfectly wholesome, parents nevertheless have to worry about the part that isn't appropriate. This disturbing trend signifies that parents can no longer be confident that their children will not have access to dark violence, sexual innuendo or offensive language on entertainment programming targeted toward children.[50]

The PTC analysis covered a three-week period of entertainment programming for school-aged children that aired on eight networks. Nearly 3,500 incidents of violence, or an average of 7.86 instances per hour, were logged during the length of the study.[51] Another recent study shows that parents abet the problem by relying on TV as a babysitter. Vickie Rideout of the Kaiser Family Foundation, a research group that focuses on health and public-policy issues, believes parents actually use the media to help them cope in their daily lives, noting that "parents have a tough job and they rely on TV in particular to help make their lives more manageable."[52] The major Kaiser Foundation study, *The Media Family: Electronic Media in the Lives of Infants, Toddlers, Preschoolers, and Their Parents,* was based on a survey of more than a thousand parents with children ages six months to six years as well as a series of focus groups across the country. As the report notes, results showed that "electronic media is a central focus of many very young children's lives, used by parents to help manage busy schedules, keep the peace, and facilitate family routines such as eating, relaxing, and falling asleep." One in three children in the study had a television in their bedroom. Another third live in homes in which the TV is on all or most of the time. As Rideout notes, "Parents use media to help keep their kids occupied, calm them down, avoid family squabbles, and teach their kids the things parents are afraid they don't have time to teach themselves."[53] As we have seen earlier, the American Academy of Pediatrics strongly believes that children under age two should not be watching television, but the AAP does acknowledge that using education and interactive programs or videos with young children can be helpful to their mental development. Unfortunately, this is not what is happening in the majority of homes. One mother who took part in the Kaiser focus group told researchers that her life with her young son would be worse, not better, without the media. "Media make life easier. We're all happier. He isn't throwing tantrums. I can get some work done," she said.[54]

Perhaps the most pernicious effect that television has on our culture today is the general lowering of sexual mores. There are plenty of sordid examples that illustrate how television producers and executives have lowered moral standards to the point where we now are facing several societal epidemics. For example, a 2004 report by the RAND Corporation, a non-profit research group that surveyed approximately 1,800 twelve- to seventeen-year-olds found that sexually-charged television programs definitely influence teens to have sex.[55] Of course, this is not news to most, but the facts and figures provided by the research are alarming and provide good ammunition in the current war for our culture. RAND reported that teens who watched more sexual content were also more likely to initiate sexual activity and to progress to more advanced sexual acts.[56] Other studies have shown that nearly seventy percent of all television programs contain sexual content and that young people view 14,000 sexual messages each year.[57] Soap operas are twenty-four times more likely to show sexual activity between unmarried people than married couples, and young people love to watch soaps. We would have to be naïve to think there is no correlation between the plethora of provocative television programs and the rampant sexual activity in our society and among our school-aged youth. An astounding forty-seven percent of high-school students in the United States have been sexually active.[58]

I am often asked how society has arrived at the point where almost nothing is sacred on daytime soaps and prime-time programming. Deregulation in the 1980s played a part, as did the 1996 Telecommunications Act, which allowed for much of the consolidation and cross-ownership of broadcast stations that exists today. With only a handful of companies owning most of the broadcast outlets, fewer voices are involved in decision making and programming. The Second Vatican Council was well ahead of its time when, in 1963, it raised questions and concerns over such a scenario.

> How, in the face of competition to capture a large popular audience, are the media to be prevented from appealing to and inflaming the less admirable tendencies in human nature? How can one avoid the concentration of the power to communicate in too few hands, so that any real dialogue is killed?[59]

As is the case with most controversies, it all comes down to the bottom line. The name of the television game is to make the most money with the least investment in quality and creativity possible. This is why Janet Jackson's infamous "wardrobe malfunction" aired during the 2004 Super Bowl halftime show. In an effort to lock the ratings up for the entire program, CBS pushed the envelope. The network, however, got their hands singed when public outcry prompted the Federal Communications

Commission (FCC) to slap them with a half-million-dollar fine. This scare put the lion back in its cage for a short time. Broadcast outlets across the country took measures, such as issuing new guidelines, holding seminars, and re-training employees to ensure on-air personalities would comply with FCC regulations. With the passage of time, though, the media continues to push the envelope. The cultural fallout that results will also continue unless we take more aggressive steps to correct the problem.

MAKING A DIFFERENCE IN TELEVISION

Action Items

1. Keep televisions out of bedrooms. Any TVs should be in rooms accessible to the entire family.
2. Place time limits on television viewing. The American Association of Pediatrics recommends no more than two hours a day for children.
3. Avoid watching television during dinner.
4. Watch what your children are watching.
5. Be an active viewer and discuss what you are watching with your children.
6. Point out positive behaviors on television, including examples of kindness, cooperation, and friendship, and challenge negative behaviors.
7. Be a good example by monitoring your own television habits.
8. Join a media activist group.
9. Make an effort to contact program sponsors, networks, and local affiliates and tell them what you like and dislike about their programming.
10. Contact public officials, including the Federal Communications Commission, and voice your concerns about the state of television programming.

CHAPTER 9

Radio:
Trashy Airwaves Coming
to a Town near You

In honor of their friend who was about to tie the knot, several young men at a Detroit company decided to throw the groom-to-be a bachelor party complete with female strippers. On the day of the party, the guys decided to take their indecent plans a step further by inviting the exotic dancers to a game of strip poker. The scenario sounds like something that might play out in one of the basements of a few unsavory fellows, or a scene from a pornographic movie. Well, welcome to radio in the twenty-first century. Listeners tuned to a particular shock jock were treated to this bachelor party as it played out live in a radio studio. The on-air personalities spared no details as they described what the strip-poker participants were or were not wearing in the broadcast booth, as well as commentary on the strippers' body parts. Why would the station's management conclude that this was a suitable mainstream broadcast? To give context to how poor the programming judgment was, the show aired during afternoon drive time, which begins at 3:00 p.m., just in time for children to listen in after school.

Hundreds of similarly raunchy "bits" air on commercial radio stations across the country, and they have been for quite some time. As traditional broadcast radio stations compete against the Internet and satellite for a share of the ever-shrinking radio audience, the envelope is pushed further and further. In the early 1990s, a major station in one of the top five U.S. markets tried to create a stir with a promotion that centered on a female personality from their popular morning show. She had received complimentary breast implants from a cosmetic surgeon who was running ads on the station. Not only did the morning jock offer endless details about his cohost's new body, but the station also promoted a big publicity event during which she would publicly reveal her augmentation. Most of my colleagues in the media business just rolled their eyes and paid no attention to the stunt. After all, radio is "theater of the mind." The problem is that the minds of those who run stations seem to be in the gutter as they sink lower and lower in their attempts to "one-up" their competitors. According to a 1999 study, twenty-two percent of teen-oriented radio segments contained sexual content.[60] It is truly shocking what radio stations are allowed to get away with these days.

Behold, there is a line in the sand. Thanks to some over-the-top stunts that stunned even the most liberal media watchers, pressure to clean up the airwaves has started to build. In recent years, three of the most infamous shock jocks were banished to satellite radio, which does not fall under FCC control. In New York, Opie and Anthony were fired from their nationally-syndicated Infinity Broadcasting show after airing a live segment with a couple having sex in the confessional of St. Patrick's Cathedral. Howard Stern promised to get George W. Bush out of office by mounting an aggressive on-air campaign against him. Not only did Stern's ratings and publicity stunt fail, but it also upset numerous advertisers who were hit with boycotts from conservative activists. Management at Viacom, which syndicates Stern's show, began to reel him in a bit after becoming weary of the bad publicity. They were not worried about offending a few million listeners; they were worried about their bottom line. A few black eyes could prompt advertisers to pull their commercials all together. While lawmakers feebly attempt to enforce FCC indecency rules, our efforts to clean up the airwaves should concentrate on the broadcast giants' bottom lines. The effort requires tenacity. We have to address more than just the shock jocks.

If young people are not listening to the ranting and raving of Howard Stern types, then they are most likely listening to music stations that play hard rock or rap music, neither of which is made for wholesome listening. There is also a growing trend for senseless, silly, non-stop chatter on the part of morning and afternoon drive-time teams. It is important for parents and concerned citizens to become educated on the content of the airwaves. This does not mean programming the car radio's auto-select buttons to the most offensive stations, but it does mean staying informed. Several family organizations and research groups regularly track and challenge questionable content, and they regularly publish their activities and findings on their websites. Among these are the Parents Television Council (PTC), National Institute on Media, the Family Research Council, and Morality in Media. (Please see the *Your Family Media Guide* at the end of this book for more information.)

The amount of distasteful content on the airwaves, combined with the liberal slant of the secular media, has caused positive fallout in the radio industry. Numerous successful conservative talk shows, including those hosted by Sean Hannity, Rush Limbaugh, Laura Ingraham, Michael Medved, along with Protestant and Catholic radio stations and networks, have taken the airwaves by storm. In their book *America's Right Turn—How Conservatives Used New and Alternative Media to Take Power,* Richard A. Viguerie and David Frank show that talk radio, direct mail, cable TV news, and the Internet (the so-called "alternative media) continue to grow, with forty percent of Americans now getting their news from these sources.[61] Viguerie and Frank predict that sixty percent of Americans will get their news and information from these same sources by the 2008 elections.[62]

Numerous Gallup polls have demonstrated just how out of touch the so-called mainstream media is and why conservative outlets continue to gain momentum. One such poll showed the average American is now much more likely to identify himself as conservative or moderate rather than liberal. Forty percent of Americans now describe themselves as conservative, and another forty percent describe themselves as moderate. Only twenty percent consider themselves to be liberal.[63] Much mainstream radio programming, though, does not seem to reflect these statistics. Is it any wonder that radio as a whole—with the exception of talk radio—has fewer listeners today compared to years past?

At present, there are nearly 130 Catholic radio stations in the United States. Although this count is small in comparison to the number of secular stations, the figure has almost doubled since the year 2000. More importantly, the impact and reach of these stations is clearly growing. There is also a genuine movement among lay Catholics to pool resources and buy full-power secular stations and convert them to a Catholic format. Networks such EWTN Radio, Ave Maria Radio, Relevant Radio, and Immaculate Heart Radio are just a few of the successful, multi-station Catholic outlets on the air today. However, most Catholic radio stations non-profit enterprises and depend on public radio-style financial model. Thus, they are not dependent upon advertisers but rely on listener support. In order to remain on the air, these outlets must undertake the arduous task of annual fund raising. On the upside, though, since non-profit stations do not have to woo advertisers with ratings figures, they have no need to subscribe to Arbitron, the industry's leading ratings provider. As a result, we do not truly know the extent of the impact they are having on secular radio. Ever wonder why many of the AM stations that were so hot in the 1960s and '70s now air religious programming? The answer is simple. Christian radio serves a niche and makes money, which means it appeals to listeners and sponsors who are not buying into secular radio.

My audience tells me that when they listen to Catholic radio, they relearn the faith. As the old adage goes, *When the student is ready, the teacher will appear.* Adults tell me they find Christ's message much more relevant, and the *Catechism* is presented in a comprehensible manner on radio. In this hectic day and age, many find it helpful being able to hear solid Catholic teaching on the radio while driving or at work. Others enjoy the interaction of live talk shows. Some simply do not have time to read, which is why programs like Ave Maria Radio's *Kresta in the Afternoon* with Al Kresta, *The Catholic Connection* with yours truly, *Catholic Answers Live*, and *EWTN Live* have become so popular. Pope John Paul II obviously understood these dynamics, and that is why he strongly supported the growth of Catholic radio, stating, "Radio may well be the most cost effective means of reaching large numbers of people who may not want to read or may lack exposure to Catholic publications, but will be willing to 'eavesdrop' on Catholic radio stations or programming."[64]

Pope John Paul II also understood radio's potential as a valuable tool for effective evangelization.

> Radio may offer perhaps the closest equivalent today to what Jesus was able to do with large groups through his preaching. Radio is an intimate medium which can reach people on the street in their cars or in their homes.[65]

As the Holy Father notes, radio offers intimate, one-on-one communication. Most people are alone in their cars, at their desks, or at home when they listen. Despite the distasteful content cluttering our airwaves, John Paul II never gave up on the media. In fact, he seemed to imply that the Lord Himself might make use of this medium if He were walking the earth today.

MAKING A DIFFERENCE IN RADIO

Action Items

1. Pray for the continued growth of Catholic radio outlets.
2. Support religious radio through financial contributions.
3. Become familiar with programs currently running on secular airwaves.
4. Find out what programs and stations your children are listening to.
5. Keep certain radio programs or stations off-limits to children and explain the reasons behind this decision.
6. Write to program directors and general managers at secular radio stations as well as Catholic and family-friendly stations to express your concerns about and interests in certain programming.
7. Contact advertisers who sponsor distasteful programs and voice your concern.
8. Put your money where your mouth is by participating in boycotts.
9. Support legislation to increase broadcast indecency fines.
10. Contact public officials and the FCC when a program offends your faith or sensibilities.

CHAPTER 10

The Internet:
Connected to Techno Trouble

Imagine being a happily married woman who, out of the blue one day, discovers that the man she thought was an upstanding devoted husband has an addiction to child pornography. Or imagine the devastation of learning that your teenage daughter distributed suggestive pictures of herself over the Internet via a webcam in her bedroom? Finally, imagine you are in the awkward early teen years and the camaraderie and friendship you thought you found through Internet chat turned into unimaginable abuse and exploitation.

The situations described above are real. They involve actual people whose stories made headlines. The woman who discovered her husband's illicit viewing habits came from an upscale suburban Detroit neighborhood. A friend she had called to fix the family computer found the child pornography. The wife knew she had to turn the evidence over to police.

The case of the mom whose daughter plastered her own image on the Internet did not make the front pages, but it did make it to police stations. Sheriff Michael Bouchard of Oakland County, Michigan spoke about the case with me for a story I wrote in Detroit's *Metro Parent Magazine*. The sheriff, who eight years earlier had started a computer-crimes unit to deal with increasing Internet problems, regularly conducts Internet safety seminars. "This mom was actually in one of our classes," Bouchard said. "She took our lessons to heart. Some of the skills she learned enabled her to discover that her daughter had been involved with a predator using her webcam."[66]

The third and most alarming case came to light in March 2006 when Justin Berry, a teenager from California, shocked his family and the world with his testimony before Congress. He was a lonely boy who thought the Internet would be a good place to make friends. Instead, he became the victim of sexual abuse. "At thirteen, I believed these people were my friends," he said. "They were kind. They complimented me. They wanted to know about my day." Berry went on to describe how drugs, sex, and money would soon dominate his life. Because of these relationships and the easy opportunity offered by the Web, he soon became an Internet porn star. According to Berry, it was easy to get started. One of his on-line "friends" lent him the money to purchase a web cam. He later made thousands of dollars by posting pictures of himself on the Internet. Members of the congressional panel may have been sickened by his testimony, but Berry made sure they understood that his case was not unique. He told them, "This is not, as many want to believe, the story of a few bad kids whose parents paid no attention. There are hundreds of kids in the United States wrapped up in this horror."[67] Justin is right on both accounts. Lawmakers, parents, teachers, and the rest of us want to believe this type of horror happens only occasionally, but as Justin pointed out, that is simply not the case. While I may hear more Internet horror stories than the average person because of my line of work, the reality is that be it home, school, work, or other social settings, we are all in close proximity to someone who struggles with Internet issues. We simply may not be aware of it, as Bishop Paul S. Loverde of Arlington, Virginia, stresses in his recent pastoral letter on the evils of pornography.

> Young Christians struggle to live the demands of discipleship amid the pressures of the surrounding culture. This process of integration becomes more difficult in a culture which, over the last generation, has abandoned the virtue of chastity.
>
> Spouses—especially husbands—striving to grow in the fidelity inherent in their marital vocation, encounter temptations to escape and seek false comfort in images and fantasies.
>
> Priests and religious, having committed themselves to a chaste and celibate life, find themselves in the midst of a culture that views celibacy as an impossible and even unhealthy goal. In moments of doubt, they may reach out for the false comforts of impurity. Their failure is all the more grave because of the scandal it brings to the Church.

> Single men and women are distracted by these
> fantasies from their most important task of discerning
> God's call in their life. In moving from impure
> thoughts to images to actual sexual misconduct,
> they undermine the foundation of trust and fidelity
> required for future happiness.
>
> No person living in our culture can totally separate
> himself or herself from the scourge of pornography.
> All are affected to a greater or lesser extent, even
> those who do not directly participate in the use of
> pornography. Yet if those who have given in to this
> vice were to answer honestly whether pornography
> made them happier or better persons, only the
> most dismissive would answer "yes." An honest
> assessment reveals that the use of pornography is
> debilitating spiritually, socially and emotionally.[68]

A report by the non-profit activist group Common
Sense Media found that eighty percent of parents are
worried about their kids encountering predators online.
The same study shows parents recognize that the Internet
can be an important tool in their children's lives. Ninety-
one percent of the parents polled in the Common Sense
survey said the Internet "helps their children expand their
passions."[69] Respondents also praised the Internet as an
educational tool, but saw a need for more education and
more parental control. Most astonishing is the paradox
between parents' knowledge of potential problems and
their weak attempts to monitor this medium. Eighty-eight
percent of the respondents surveyed said it was imperative
that parents have a grip on what their children do on-
line.[70] So why is it that day after day, we hear stories about
seemingly clueless parents discovering that children are
mixed up with dangerous characters on the Internet?

One of the most shocking cases involved a teen from Saginaw, Michigan who ended up in Amman, Jordan with a man she met through MySpace.com in June 2006. The girl told her parents that she wanted to go on vacation with her friend's family. So mom got the girl a passport and drove her daughter to the bus station in Saginaw. When the friend's family never showed, mom called them and learned that no vacation had been planned. The mother promptly brought her daughter home, but the next day the girl's parents awoke to find her missing. On her own, she jetted off to the Middle East with a stranger. She called home three times but didn't reveal that she was halfway around the world—and in the Middle East of all places! According to her mother, the girl was a member of the National Honor Society and she never gave the family any trouble. Her heavy involvement with the Internet seriously impaired her judgment.

A recent Pew Internet Project study found that eighty-seven percent of all youth between the ages of twelve and seventeen use the Internet. That translates to about twenty-one million teenagers. These figures have grown rapidly and continue to increase.[71] It is frightening to think of how many young people log onto the Web unsupervised or under-supervised by parents who grant liberal surfing habits. A 2005 Kaiser Family Foundation survey of more than two thousand third- through twelfth-graders found that, despite warnings from public officials and law enforcement agencies, the majority of parents do not set or enforce rules for Internet use.[72]

According to the National Center for Missing and Exploited Children, parents might take a proactive approach to their children's Internet habits if they fully realized that sites like MySpace.com and Facebook.com, which attract teens and pre-teens alike, are also one-stop shopping opportunities for pedophiles. One in five children in the United States has received a sexual solicitation from an Internet chat room. Law enforcement agencies estimate that at any given time, there are fifty thousand predators on-line in this country. Attorneys general in three states have investigated cases of child sexual abuse and statutory rape involving young people who were assaulted by older men they met on-line.[73] While most parents would not let their underage kids wander the streets alone at night, surveys show that more than thirty-one percent of America's teens have unmonitored Internet access in their bedrooms.[74]

An information-technology professional I interviewed for my newspaper column offered this analogy, "Parents who grant their children unmonitored Internet access might as well leave their front doors wide open for strangers at night when they go to bed."[75] Many stories of child abductions involving pedophiles have begun with relationships forged on the Internet. Like that of Justin Berry, case after case involves underage children who are easily persuaded to divulge personal information. Children convince parents that the sites they visit are secure and that no one can access their personal profiles without having first been given their password. What children fail to explain, or perhaps are unaware of themselves, is that they do not always know the person with whom they are sharing information. Predators are expert con artists who lie about their identities and invest as much time as needed to earn their prey's trust.

Ken Henderson is a convert to Catholicism and a former porn addict who now runs a growing apostolate that helps men overcome sexual addictions. Henderson says parents are, for the most part, clueless when it comes to what he calls the "extreme danger" in which their children may be when they visit MySpace and Facebook.

> Aside from the frequent pornographic material that can be found on these sites, there is also the predator element. Because it is an on-line community, people who post to the site are not always who they say they are and, thus, young people can be easily deceived by sexual predators posing as teens themselves. There is the very real possibility of a teen or pre-teen being lured into sexual exploitation or worse.[76]

Henderson offers the following suggestions:

> It is absolutely imperative that parents know where their children are going on the web. Parents need to maintain the home computer in a center location in the home and children should never have a computer with Internet access in the privacy of their bedrooms. Also, accountability software like Safe Eyes (www.SafeEyes.com) and Covenant Eyes (www.CovenantEyes.com) are a must if you want to monitor every web site that is accessed on their

computer. Parents must be diligent to insure their
children do not end up getting trapped in a world
of pornography that can easily lead to addiction
and a distortion of sex, the human person, and the
family.[77]

Teenagers are not the only group poised to encounter
Internet tribulations. Countless adults are plagued with on-
line temptations. Delving into pornography once involved
making considerable efforts, taking risks, and may have
involved traveling to a seedy part of town. Not any more.
Thanks to wireless networks, sophisticated cell phones,
personal digital assistants (PDAs) and other hi-tech
devices, the Internet is available just about anywhere and
to anyone. Likewise, explicit images are readily available.
A businessman can view a little porn on his laptop or
Blackberry as he sips his coffee on the train ride into work,
and no one has to know. A teenager can beam images to a
friend's cell phone during algebra class. The opportunities
are endless, and the temptation to indulge is pervasive.

In an effort to prevent parents from buying their
children cell phones, iPods, and other Internet-capable
gadgets for Christmas, William Cardinal Keeler, Archbishop
of Baltimore, warned parents about "a perfect storm of
pornography" that was headed our way in a statement
he issued prior to the 2005 Christmas shopping season.[78]
(He issued a similar warning again during the same time
period of 2006.) As an active member of the Religious
Alliance against Pornography, Cardinal Keeler faces down

a wealthy, many-headed monster in the porn industry. Pornographers generate between ten and twenty billion dollars annually from Internet porn sites, pornographic magazines, and videos.[79] An estimated 200,000 Americans are seeking professional help for cybersex addictions.[80] The issue is being addressed regularly at marriage seminars and in marriage-counseling sessions. Friends and colleagues of mine who work with engaged and married couples through Worldwide Marriage Encounter and National Marriage Encounter say the topic of sexual impurity resulting from Internet porn surfaces frequently. A survey of men who attend the well-known Promise Keepers conferences held around the country each year showed that more than fifty percent admit that they are in a spiritual battle for sexual purity.[81] John Paul II was on target when he warned about the dangers of the Internet, explaining that it can easily add to the idea of moral relativism so prevalent in today's society:

> And when values are disregarded, our very humanity is demeaned and man easily loses sight of his transcendent dignity....Moreover, as a forum in which practically everything is acceptable and almost nothing is lasting, the Internet favors a relativistic way of thinking and sometimes feeds the flight from personal responsibility and commitment.[82]

Two other areas of serious concern regarding children and the Internet are cyber bullying and the continued dumbing down of our culture through the growing use of on-line lingo. Cyber bullying has made headlines across the country. In short, victims are the subject of cruel e-mails, text messages, blog posts, etc. The March 21, 2005 issue of *People* included a lengthy story about a boy who committed suicide after being teased on-line. A March 2005 *USA Today* cover story highlighted the growing trend of this type of bullying. According to a 2001 survey by the Kaiser Family Foundation and Nickelodeon, seventy-four percent of eight- to eleven-year-olds say teasing and bullying occur at their school. More recently, a story on CBS' *The Early Show*, revealed that some forty percent of students claimed to have been bullied on-line. Many of the perpetrators of school shooting incidents in the United States had been victims of bullying or harassment, including the gunman in the March 2005 Red Lake Reservation massacre in Minnesota. The perpetrator shot and killed nine people, including his own grandfather, and injured more than a dozen others before taking his own life.

The normally quiet and quaint Amish community of Lancaster County, Pennsylvania was rocked by a violent and deadly school massacre on October 2, 2006. The gunman, thirty-two-year-old Charles Carl Roberts IV, killed five girls between the ages of seven and thirteen before taking his own life in the one-room Amish schoolhouse. Roberts' suicide note indicated that he was acting on a grudge that he had held for twenty years. The nature of the grudge had not been divulged, but we do know that it began at the impressionable and challenging age of twelve—the age at which many middle-school harassments are leveled.

Whether they realize it or not, droves of Internet users—especially young people—are part of a new subculture, the downfall of which is jargon that is practically becoming a language unto itself. Codes and acronyms abound in this cyber language. The problem is that even though these codes do not translate well into spoken words, they are slowly being incorporated into everyday speech, creating yet another generational gap as well as a challenge in the classroom. Aside from innocent abbreviations like: BBL ("be back later"), BO ("brain overload") and LOL ("laughing out loud"), numerous codes are being used to bully, gossip, and talk about sex on-line. Connect with Kids and other Internet safety sites point out the dangers of such language, which is generally understood by kids and predators alike.

Educators say our media subculture negatively affects students' academic performance. Researchers at New York's Albert Einstein College issued a report in November 2006 which confirmed the need for students to turn off the computer, television, radio, and other media devices and focus more on their studies. The study, involving more than four thousand middle-school students, demonstrated that the more time a student spends on-line, playing video games, or watching television, the lower his or her grades.[83] Many teachers notice a decline in the aptitude of high-school students, whose writings increasingly include incorrect grammar and abbreviations and whose papers are devoid of detailed descriptions, resulting in lower standardized test scores.[84] A 2003 Jupiter Research study found that seventy percent of teens said instant messaging was their favorite on-line activity.[85]

Take heart. As with television and radio, the Internet can be a great source for information and, even more importantly, a great tool for evangelization. Remember that charming footage of Pope John Paul II sitting behind a desk at the Vatican's Clementine Hall in 2001? He was captured hitting the "send" button on his laptop, firing off an e-mail in the process. While the press might have considered it a good photo op, the gesture meant much more to the Pope and to countless Catholic evangelists. This simple act was, in a sense, the "baptizing" of a new means of evangelization. John Paul II also wanted the ability to reach as many of his flock as possible and to afford them an opportunity to reach him. The plan worked. According to an Associated Press report, in March 2005, the Vatican received more than ten thousand e-mails in English and six thousand in Spanish for the ailing Pontiff. Even the announcement of the Pope's death came from the new medium as the Vatican press office issued an e-mail alert to the media. In 1989, when personal computers and laptops were still a new reality, and e-mail accounts and the Internet were not yet in the average American's lexicon, John Paul called on the universal Church to harness the computer culture for the sake of the Gospel. His concerns were addressed that year in his World Communications Day letter:

> It is clear that the Church must also avail herself of the new resources provided by human exploration in computer and satellite technology for her ever-pressing task of evangelization. Her most vital and urgent message has to do with knowledge of Christ and the way of salvation, which He offers.[86]

John Paul II saw the Internet as a way to reach those who had been unreachable or difficult to reach.

> With each day that passes, the vision of earlier years becomes ever more a reality. It was a vision which foresaw the possibility of real dialogue between widely separated peoples, of a worldwide sharing of ideas and aspirations of growth in mutual knowledge and understanding, of a strengthening of brotherhood across many hitherto insurmountable barriers.[87]

In the first years of his pontificate, Pope Benedict XVI appears to be following the example of his predecessor by using the media, including the Internet, as a means of communicating with his worldwide flock. The Vatican has an updated and upgraded website, making the teachings of the Church as well as the writings of the Holy Father accessible to every one. "Do not be overcome by evil, but overcome evil with good" (Romans 12:21). Like television, there is both value and danger in the use of the Internet. The Internet can also be a force for good. So, let's not throw the baby out with the bathwater, but do proceed with caution.

MAKING A DIFFERENCE ON THE INTERNET

Action Items

1. Keep computers with Internet access out of children's bedrooms.
2. Keep a computer with Internet access in a central area of the home such as the kitchen or family room.
3. Place time limits on computer and Internet usage.
4. Monitor the websites your children are visiting.
5. Spend time with children on the Internet so you can set a positive example.
6. Talk with family members about possible on-line dangers including cyber bullying, and sexual solicitations.
7. Remind children to never give out personal information on-line.
8. Monitor your own computer habits.
9. Subscribe to family-friendly Internet Service Providers (ISPs).
10. Make use of Internet blocking programs and filters.

CHAPTER 11

Music and Music Videos: Cranial Pollution & The Cerebral Arcade

"I want to talk to the black men in here, you know what I mean?
Black men in here that are coming up in the hood, coming up in
the struggle. We're killing each other, dawg. You feel me? You know?
And it's about nothing, it's about nothing. Nothing."

Obie Trice offered the above dissertation at the April 2006 funeral of his friend, fellow rapper Proof. Trice's statement was quoted in the *Detroit News* and in various other sources. Proof was yet another murder victim from the violent world of rap music—an art form that all too often appears to imitate life. A host of major hip-hop stars packed Detroit's Fellowship Chapel to say goodbye to their friend, whose real name was DeShaun Holton. Holton was gunned down during a shootout over a game of pool in an after-hours club. According to police reports, Holton was the first to open fire. In addition to Trice, ministers at Proof's funeral also pleaded for a ceasefire in our inner cities. Thousands of fans that stood outside the Motor City church lamented the senseless violence, telling reporters that it had to stop. However, no one—not the religious leaders, rappers, or fans—called for an end to the violent lyrics and messages in rap music. Only a few columnists had the guts to point out the hypocrisy of the situation.

Trice had been the victim of a shooting four months earlier on New Year's Eve, 2005. He was hit twice, with one of the bullets piercing his head, as he drove on a Detroit freeway. Although Trice survived the gunfire, the bullet that struck his head remained lodged there, as doctors feared it would be too dangerous to operate. Despite his own experience and the passionate plea he made at his buddy's funeral, Trice continues to record lyrics with violent themes. He can barely get through a sentence without spewing foul language, making angry threats, or denigrating women with disgusting and offensive verbiage. (Trice's controversial rap lyrics, which are heard by hundreds of thousands of teens across the country, can be read on line at www.lyrics.com.) We simply cannot have it both ways. We cannot call for change but continue to promote and support violence in music and the media.

A study that happened to be released within a week of Proof's death revealed an alarming connection between rap music and drugs, alcohol, and violence. Scientists at the Pacific Institute for Research and Evaluation surveyed more than one thousand community college students and found that rap music was "consistently associated with alcohol use, potential alcoholism, illicit drug use, and aggressive behavior."[88] The study's lead author, Meng-Jinn

Chen, issued a written statement addressing the cause for concern.

> People should be concerned about rap and hip-hop being used to market alcoholic beverages, given the alcohol, drug and aggression problems among listeners. That's particularly true considering the popularity of rap and hip-hop among young people. …While we don't fully understand the relationship between music preferences and behavioral outcomes, our study shows that young people may be influenced by frequent exposure to music lyrics that make positive references to substance use and violence.[89]

As if the battle taking place in headsets, laptops, and car radios were not enough, today's teens also face a barrage of moral challenges from music videos. A 2004 Parents Television Council (PTC) survey found that seventy-three percent of American boys and seventy-eight percent of American girls between the ages of twelve and nineteen regularly watch MTV.[90] During 171 hours of programming, content aired on MTV showed 1,548 sexual scenes containing 3,056 depictions of sex or various forms of nudity, 2,881 verbal references to sex, and six instances of violence per hour.[91]

Fortunately, there is resistance from some within the secular media. The editors of *Essence* magazine have expressed remorse and outrage over the way black women are typically portrayed in hip-hop and rap videos. The publication, which is marketed to African American women, has a paid circulation of nearly one million readers.

In January 2005, *Essence* launched "Take Back the Music," a year-long campaign opposing sexually-charged images in music videos. *Essence* fashion and beauty manager Michaela Angela Davis said, "It's a big family problem that needs intervention. We are coming at this from a place of concern, as opposed to taking up picket signs, because it is a complicated issue. We are not telling people what to think, but we are telling them to think."[92] During the course of the campaign, representatives from *Essence* met with various hip-hop and rap artists to encourage them to express their music in manners that reflect a positive image of women.

Efforts to disassociate from mainstream rap stars are further evidence of the disdain for the offensive blatant messages in their music. In protest of Nelly's controversial video "Tip Drill," Atlanta's Spellman College rescinded an invitation to have the rap star appear on campus. The video includes a highly offensive scene of Nelly swiping a credit card down a woman's backside. The college was smart to distance itself from any relationship that might have been construed as condoning vile behavior. Such forms of so-called entertainment still have plenty of sponsors in other arenas to keep them profitable. It is essential, therefore, that we monitor what our children watch as well as the choices we make for ourselves. The limits of decency are being pushed in all forms of visual entertainment in a trend known as the "ratings creep."

A July 2004 study by the Harvard School of Public Health and the Kids Risk Project found that violence, profanity, and sexual contact increased greatly in movies made between 1992 and 1993. Movies that were rated R (restricted to those over age seventeen) twenty-five years ago are rated PG-13 (parental guidance for anyone under age thirteen) today. Although it is public knowledge, many are not aware that the ratings system is voluntary and that it is the Motion Picture Association of America (MPAA), the official lobbying arm of the film industry, that tags movies with content ratings. If this sounds self-serving on the part of Hollywood producers, that's because it is. In addition, many R-rated films are marketed to an audience that, according to their ratings, is too young to view them. A Federal Trade Commission report to Congress revealed that the motion picture industry advertises and promotes R-rated films in media and venues popular with young people.[93]

Films that are supposed to be kid-friendly often send out wrong messages. In March 2004, a joint effort by the American Academy of Pediatrics, the Campaign for Tobacco Free Kids, American Legacy Foundation, and Smoke-Free Movies aimed to draw attention to the amount of smoking in films. According to the groups' research, eighty percent of PG-13 films featured some form of tobacco use, while fifty percent of G- and PG-rated movies depicted smoking. So we cannot expect much help from Hollywood. These are the same folks who attacked Mel Gibson's blockbuster epic film *The Passion of the Christ* for being too violent, yet praised the blood and gore in films like *The Gladiator.*

In light of the extraordinary success of *The Passion*, many wonder why Hollywood shows little interest in producing more overtly religious films. In April 2005, I had the chance to conduct a radio interview with Gavin Palone, the executive producer of the NBC series *Revelations.* Palone explained that Hollywood executives are ignorant of the concerns of the majority of our population, and they underestimate the number of faithful in this country. Palone stressed the importance of the public's support for films, television programs, and other forms of entertainment that spread a positive faith message because Hollywood will only get the message when it is spoken in the language they understand best—money.

As with the vast majority of professionals in the news and information industry, most Hollywood executives and producers profess to be either atheist or agnostic, have little interest in religious topics, are extremely liberal in their political preferences, and assume the majority of consumers think as they do (or at least that they *should* think the same way). The Hollywood power brokers cannot quite figure out what is going on in "fly over" country, i.e., all those "red" states between the East and West Coasts. They seem to ignore all the research that shows we live in a very religious country. Some evidence: an April 2005

Barna Research Group study found that more than ninety percent of American adults engage in some type of faith-related practice in the course of a typical week.[94] Barna's State of the Church, 2005, report also found a significant increase in Bible reading, with forty-five percent of adults reading the Scriptures on a weekly basis. So Hollywood is not quite in step with the "real" America.

To understand the motivation that fuels Hollywood, simply review the history of Academy Award nominations. *The Passion of the Christ,* despite being one of the most popular films of all time and grossing more than $370 million in the United States alone, was passed over for most of the major categories in 2004 and failed to take home Oscars in the two categories it was nominated, best cinematography and best musical score. The big winners in 2005, *Million Dollar Baby* and *Vera Drake*, were films that glamorized euthanasia and abortion, respectively.

Another billion-dollar entertainment medium in need of a lasso is video games. Video-game revenues hit twenty billion dollars worldwide in the year 2000. This is a huge enterprise that spews out more of the same garbage we discussed earlier, and it is aimed directly at our children. According to the National Institute on Media and the Family, sixty-seven percent of households with children own a video game system. Consider the ages of family members most likely to use those systems, and then consider the fact that a large number of M-rated (i.e., for mature audiences) games target children under the age of seventeen.[95] According to the National Institute on Media and the Family, fifty percent of fourth graders in this country prefer first-person shooter video games. First-person shooter (FPS) simulates the in-game character's point of view and focuses on the use of handheld weaponry. The same study by the Institute also found that playing violent video games on a regular basis could increase aggressive thoughts by forty-three percent.[96] Some of the best-selling games on the market right now include *Doom 3*, *Grand Theft Auto: San Andreas*, and *Resident Evil: Outbreak*. Each is rated M and contains plenty of violence and sexual content, and although they have been "kid-tested," none are "mother-approved." The National Institute on Media and the Family noted the mixed message delivered by the video-game industry, which tells parents to pay attention to the ratings on its games but also denies that its products are harmful.[97]

It is no secret that our children and young adults are influenced by their most universal means of entertainment: music, video images, and video games. They are near and dear to our teens' hearts. So for us this means extra vigilance and patience in trying to guide their entertainment choices. In addition to the following suggestions, the action steps suggested in previous chapters can also be applied here.

MAKING A DIFFERENCE IN MUSIC, MUSIC VIDEOS, AND VIDEO GAMES

Action Items

1. Develop firm and clear media guidelines concerning the acceptable content of music, music videos, and video games.
2. Explain why particular messages or themes are unacceptable.
3. Do your homework. Do not rely entirely on the current industry rating systems.
4. Keep video-game players out of children's bedrooms.
5. Visit Christian and other family-friendly web sites for content information as well as entertainment ideas, such as Kids-in-Mind. com.
6. Review the lyrics and messages before purchasing music selections.
7. Introduce yourself and your family to a wide range of music.
8. Flex your financial muscle by not purchasing products that do not promote moral values.
9. Check with local theatres to see if they follow movie ratings guidelines.
10. Avoid first-person shooter and M-rated video games.

CHAPTER 12

Advertising:
Paying For Propaganda

Try as we might, we simply cannot dodge all the messages aimed at us. Want proof? Take this advertising quiz:

1. Name the tiger that has been telling us for decades that his cereal is *grrrreat!*
2. Which athletic gear company has encouraged us to "Just do it?"
3. Name the cigarette brand that told women in the 1970s, "You've come a long way baby."

The point is that advertising works. Popular conservative talk-show host Michael Medved once said that if the media do not have an impact on society, then everyone on Madison Avenue should turn off the lights and go home. If media had no effect on what we buy, eat, or think, why would companies like Kellogg's, Nike, and good ol' Virginia Slims spend millions on broadcast, print, and Internet ads?

Corporate America understands the benefits of advertising, but advertising requires making an investment.

Companies therefore need to budget their advertising dollars carefully. They research the best methods for appropriating ad dollars as well as which demographics to best target their message. As our country becomes wealthier, the "money demographic" expands—that is, a wider range of consumers now has disposable income. Now more than ever, those demographics include young adults and teenagers. Teenage Research Unlimited found that in 2004 youth between the ages of twelve and nineteen spent more than $169 billion dollars.[98] The March 7, 2005 *Broadcasting and Cable* cover story "What a Teen Wants: How TV Chases an Elusive Demo" claimed that "certain advertisers, movie studios, cosmetic firms, and electronics makers are perpetually desperate to get their wares in front of [teenagers]."[99] Vatican II addressed this concern in its Pastoral Instruction *Communio et Progressio: On the Means of Social Communication*.

If harmful or utterly useless goods are touted to the public, if false assertions are made about the goods for sale, if less admirable human tendencies are exploited, those responsible for such advertising harm society and forget their good name and credibility.[100]

From television and radio to newspapers and billboards, advertisers constantly push products that claim to have the answer to all of our woes, especially our collective battle of the bulge. Total annual revenue from diet-related advertising adds up to more than thirty billion dollars.[101]

According to this organization and others, one out of every four television commercials pertains to physical attractiveness, the average American child sees as many as forty thousand television commercials every year, and young children cannot distinguish between commercials and actual programs.

Because of the TV-induced eating disorder I experienced as a child, I have little tolerance for those who are in denial about the impact the media has on our lives. The force is much greater today than it was thirty or forty years ago simply because we are inundated by media. Although we are all consumers, it is ironic to note the recent rash of celebrities whose obsessions with image have caused them to compromise their health. Modern teen stars such as Mary-Kate Olsen, one-half of the billionaire Olsen twins, reality TV's Nicole Richie, and movie star Kate Bosworth are not immune to cultural influences. The three are just a sampling of celebrities whose eating disorders have made national headlines.

According to an article in the April 2002 issue of *Health*, thirty-two percent of female network TV characters are underweight.[102] Various factors contribute to the development of eating disorders, but pressure brought on by the media's distorted image of normal ranks atop the list. The results of a 2004 study on body image and the media, which was conducted by the makers of Dove Soap, are particularly disconcerting. *The Real Truth about*

Beauty survey of more than ten thousand women in the United States, Canada, the United Kingdom, China, Brazil, and other countries found that only two percent of the respondents considered themselves beautiful. More than two-thirds agreed that the media and advertising set an unrealistic goal or standard of beauty, which most women could never achieve.[103] Is it any wonder that the amount of plastic surgery being performed on young people is reaching epidemic proportions? *Family Circle* examined the issue in an article titled "The Plastic Surgery Epidemic." It exposed startling figures from the American Society of Plastic Surgeons, which recorded nearly 3,400 breast augmentations on women eighteen years old and younger in 2003, compared to 978 girls a decade earlier.[104] With programs such as *Nip and Tuck* and *Dr. 90210* achieving cult-like status over the past few years, these numbers are surely going to go through the roof.

The impact advertising has on underage drinking is also a huge concern and has been for some time. The American Academy of Pediatrics claims that television advertising alone changes attitudes about drinking. In a 2001 report, the AAP found that after viewing alcohol ads, young people had more positive feelings about drinking. The same study found that fifty-six percent of students in grades five through twelve admit that alcohol ads encourage them to drink.[105] AAP research also found that, on average, American children view at least two thousand beer and wine commercials every year.[106] The Center for Science in the Public Interest reports that the beer industry alone spent more than $770 million on TV ads and $15 million on radio ads in 2000.[107] As a whole, the alcohol industry spends an average of two billion dollars annually on print and broadcast advertising.[108]

Meanwhile, the Center on Alcohol Marketing to Youth (CAMY) at Georgetown University found that alcohol advertising on television has grown substantially over the last several years.[109] The CAMY, which regularly monitors the advertising practices of the alcohol business, found the total number of alcohol ads on local, cable, and network TV jumped forty-one percent. In its report released in December of 2006, *Still Growing After All These Years; Youth Exposure to Alcohol Ads on TV, 2001-2005*, CAMY found America's teenagers saw an average of 217 ads in 2001 and 309 such ads in 2005. The Center's study analyzed 1.4 million alcohol ads placed on broadcast, cable and local TV at a cost of nearly $4.7 billion dollars over the four-year time period. David Jernigan, executive director of CAMY, said the alcohol industry is not getting the message that it needs to do a better job at protecting young people. "More spending on television, especially on cable translates into kids seeing more and more alcohol ads. Twenty state attorneys general and the Institute of Medicine have said that the alcohol industry needs to do a better job of shielding our kids from its advertising."[110]

The CAMY has valid cause for concern as research continues to show that underage drinking is still a major problem in this country. In January, the Centers for Disease Control and Prevention issued a new study which found that nearly half of all high-school students admitted recently to drinking alcohol with sixty-four percent of them describing themselves as binge drinkers, consuming five or more drinks in a row. The survey also found that those calling themselves binge drinkers were more likely to engage in other risky behavior including premarital sex, fighting, smoking cigarettes, and using drugs.[111]

"Get 'em young and get 'em hooked" appears to be the rallying cry of the advertising industry, and billions of dollars are being spent to ensure that success. Despite being banned from television and radio decades ago, cigarette advertising remains a viable business. The six leading cigarette makers spent more than twelve billion dollars on advertising in 2002, an eleven percent increase over the year before, according to the Federal Trade Commission (FTC).[112] The American Cancer Society reports that "nearly all first use of tobacco occurs before high school graduation and that fifty-four percent of high school students had tried smoking at some point."[113] The younger people are when they begin smoking, the more likely they are to become strongly addicted to nicotine. Worse yet, teens who smoke are three times more likely than non-smokers to use alcohol, eight times more likely to use marijuana, and twenty-two times more likely to use cocaine.

Equally detrimental to the health of individuals and society is the business of violence. Since the recent and rapid increase of school shooting incidents, the FTC has been studying the issue of marketing violent products and games to young people. The FTC tracks advertising placed in media outlets popular with young people and reviews the marketing plans for R and PG-13-rated movies, explicit-content-labeled music, and mature-rated video games. In a July 2004 report, the FTC noted some progress in providing rating information in ads, improvements in limiting sales of R-rated movie tickets to minors, and a decrease in the advertising of parental advisory-labeled music in teen magazines, but little change overall in ad placements.[114]

The FTC found that the movie, music, and video-game industries continue to advertise violent and explicit movies, games, and music in media widely watched by teens.[115] Findings in the 2004 FTC report also concluded:

- Studios continue to advertise violent films on television shows watched by audiences with large numbers of teens.
- The music industry continues to market music with explicit content on television shows viewed by large numbers of teens.
- Eighty-three percent of teen shoppers are still able to buy explicit-content labeled music.

- Ads for M-rated video games continue to appear in game enthusiast magazines popular with teens and pre-teens

One of the more annoying aspects of this advertising is the ads themselves. How many times have you had to quickly reach for the remote and switch stations to avoid embarrassment or to shield your children from inappropriate ads? A caller to my radio show described how on several occasions he dashed for the TV remote to spare his young boys provocative or otherwise inappropriate commercials only to actually attract more attention to the spots. In hindsight, he realized that had he not drawn attention to the commercials, his children might have been less affected by the indoctrinating message that a woman's value comes primarily when she is sultry. He just wished he didn't have to face such mental wrangling while his kids were still so young.

I have heard from people who say they cannot even walk through shopping malls without feeling offended by retailers like Abercrombie & Fitch and Victoria's Secret. While there's nothing inherently wrong with undergarments, objectifying women is a huge problem, as are the low self-worth issues that often result from the glorification of sex. Both clothing retailers have been taken to task in recent years for their sexually explicit print ads. Abercrombie & Fitch received so much pressure over its Christmas catalogue in 2003 that it pulled plans for a similar print promotion. These and other retailers set the trend for youth fashion (or lack thereof). Tight shirts, pants that drop well below the waist, short shorts, and accessories capable of setting off metal detectors are being marketed to children and pre-teens, not to older college students. The frustration over the push for provocative clothing has prompted many to push right back. One high-school teen made headlines in recent years when she took on Nordstrom by complaining about the lack of tasteful clothing for young girls. Management read her letters and took the young girl up on her suggestions to also offer a variety of modest clothing for girls in her age group.[116] Another positive response is the increasing popularity of the Challenge Clubs and their Pure Fashion events. Pure Fashion is an international faith-based program designed to help girls from eighth through twelfth grades rediscover and reaffirm their innate value and authentic femininity. Their website, www.purefashionshow.org, offers guidelines for appropriate dress that rival the suggestive garb being promoted in the mass media. Pure Fashion Show organizers aim to prove that it is possible to be stylish, cute, and modest. Their motto is, "Where values and virtues are always in vogue." Now, there's a concept worth promoting, huh?

Last, but certainly not least, advertising has played an immeasurable role in fueling the materialistic yearnings of millions. We simply cannot live with out the big house, fancy cars, extravagant vacations, and latest toys for the kids. The average child sees forty thousand television commercials each year. Children as young as three recognize brand logos.[117] Teen Research Unlimited found that, in 2001, teens aged twelve to nineteen spent $172 billion on consumer products. As consumer debt reaches an all-time high, so too does consumer bankruptcy. An April 15, 2005 *USA Today* cover story outlined the country's personal debt problems and quoted financial experts who recommend we go on a financial diet.[118] Jim Hicks, a financial advisor and operator of Trinity Financial, said that he comes across a number of people who have been fooled into believing we should be able to buy whatever we want even if we cannot afford it. "Materialism distracts us from our central purpose, to become Christ-like," Hicks said. According to Hicks, the average American has more than twenty-thousand dollars in credit card debt. Twenty-three percent of the average person's take home pay is committed to paying off existing debt, which does not include mortgage debt. Even among Christians, about one in seventy families have declared bankruptcy. Age and socioeconomic conditions aside, we can all use a refresher course in setting priorities as laid out for us in Scripture.

> Do not love the world or the things in the world. If any one loves the world, love for the Father is not in him. For all that is in the world, the lust of the flesh and the lust of the eyes and the pride of life is not of the Father but is of the world. And the world passes away... but he who does the will of God abides forever (1 John 2:15-17).

MAKING A DIFFERENCE IN ADVERTISING

Action Items

1. Watch television with your children and teach the family about the potential negative effects of advertising and media influence.

2. Explain the money-making motives and objectives behind advertising.

3. Watch/use age-appropriate media outlets/ products with children.

4. Discuss the false glamorization and normalization of drug and alcohol use as it is portrayed in magazines and broadcast advertisements.

5. Purchase Christian magazines as alternative reading entertainment for children and the family (see *Your Family Media Guide* at the end of the book).

6. Help children and teens find positive role models (e.g., saints, godparents, grandparents, Christian movie stars, Christian singers and songwriters).

7. Develop and encourage healthy eating habits as a family.

8. Develop and encourage your child's body image and self-esteem.

9. Contact networks, publishers, and companies about their advertising content and practices.

10. To help limit media and advertising influence, introduce a variety of activities to the family that do not involve media.

CHAPTER 13

Media Bias:
All the News That's Fit to Twist

When I think about the problem of media bias, I get frustrated. But some of the reasons for this frustration may surprise you. Yes, I am frustrated with members of my profession for not doing enough to own up to and correct the imbalance in news coverage. But I am also extremely frustrated with people of my own faith and political persuasion who do nothing but complain. When I think about media bias, I am reminded of the powerful words of Jesus in the gospel of Matthew: "Why do you see the speck that is in your brother's eye, but do not notice the log that is in your own eye?" (Matthew 7:3)

We are part of the problem; the "log" in our eyes is our silence. Though many of us may express our concerns in Catholic or conservative media outlets, we fail to speak out and challenge the secular media directly. When I ask members of my seminar audiences how many believe the news media is biased, nearly all are quick to raise their hands. But when I ask how many have met with a news director, contacted a reporter or city editor, or taken the time to write an opinion piece for the editorial section of their local newspaper, very few (if any) hands go up. When asked why, they typically respond, "Why bother"? They assume that their efforts will have little effect.

While this may be an understandable feeling, the current atmosphere will not change if Catholics do not make their voices heard. If we are willing to challenge TV entertainment executives, radio program directors, and advertising bosses about questionable content, we also need to be willing to do the same with journalists and news directors as well. You may be surprised at the results. One case in point is my home state of Michigan. The pro-life movement in Michigan, while one of the strongest in the country, has had its share of challenges from a pro-abortion governor and a liberal press. But that hasn't stopped pro-lifers from getting their voices heard in the secular media. In the final months before the midterm elections of 2006, the editorial section of major papers dedicated a large amount of their readers' response sections to those voicing concern about political coverage that failed to accurately portray the abortion issue. More recently, many of these same pro-lifers were featured in the *Detroit News*, thus allowing important points to be published, points that would never have seen the light of day without such well-crafted opinion pieces.[119]

In this chapter, we will examine the overwhelming evidence of bias in the media. The evidence is overwhelming. Though many members of the press refuse to admit bias or are in denial, the numbers don't lie: a study by the Center for Media and Public Affairs found that 2006 election coverage was bad news for the GOP and good news for the Democrats. "The tone of TV network news coverage has favored the Democratic party in this year's midterm [election]…the results are based on CMPA's scientific analysis of the 167 midterm election stories aired on the ABC, CBS, and NBC evening news between September 5th and October 22nd."[120]

It is not just the numbers in terms of how many news people lean to the left in their own political opinions; it is the numbers in terms of the studies that have been done that examine the bias in the types of interviews that are conducted, along with the types of sound bites, quotes, and headlines that are used as well as the ones that are ignored or discarded. A notorious recent example involves the way the national media let John Kerry off the hook when he made his insulting comments about troops in Iraq shortly before the midterm elections of 2006. Kerry told college students in California that if they didn't work hard in school, they would get stuck in Iraq. In the resulting controversy, the Media Research Center (MRC), a conservative think tank that monitors the media, tracked the tone of the news coverage, and it clearly demonstrated the media's political leanings: ABC News anchor Charles Gibson called it an "idle political remark," while CNN's Suzanne Malveaux commented, "We hope this all goes away tomorrow." Among the strongest reactions and most blatant bias came from CBS's Katie Couric, who actually mimicked a possible Republican television ad, saying in front of millions of viewers, "John Kerry insults troops. Do we really want the Dems to take over?"[121] MRC President L. Brent Bozell noted that the media has not been as kind to conservatives in similar situations, including Senator George Allen's "macaca" comment: "If a conservative denoted a particular group of people as stupid, these same reporters would exploit every opportunity to drive the GOP into the ground in the week before the elections. The liberal hypocrisy and media bias are loathsome."[122]

In this chapter, we will take you inside the newsrooms and show you how the media operate and think. I know because I have been there and done that and will share some personal experiences. Finally, this chapter will show that, despite how bad things are, nothing is impossible; we *can* make a difference in the news media, if we are willing to give it a try.

One of the most eye-opening conversations I had in my twenty-plus years in the secular media gave me a real perspective as to just how engrained media bias really has become in our society. The quick but revealing exchange took place between a television news executive and myself during our daily editorial meeting one day in the mid-1990s. At these meetings, producers and assignment editors prioritized story coverage and assigned particular reporters to cover them. On that particular day, some members of the local National Abortion Rights Action League (NARAL) were holding a rally and press conference to protest new pro-life efforts in Michigan. (The group has since amended its name in an effort to sound more palatable and goes by NARAL Pro-Choice America.) Knowing I had recently reverted to my Catholic faith, the news executive challenged me. In front of our staff, she said, "I know that you are pro-life. Let's see if you can be balanced and cover a NARAL event." (It was no secret that she strongly favored legalized abortion, as she had spoken candidly in the past about two abortions she'd had.) I quickly replied, "Well that's fine, but only if in all fairness, you go cover a pro-life event, being that you support legalized abortion." She was not too pleased with either my comments or my directness. Looking back, I am sure the incident had everything to do with the station's later decision not to renew my contract. At the time, though, I was beyond playing politics for the sake of my job. My convictions on this matter were strong, and my response was heartfelt. I was also not afraid to speak up for the truth and draw attention to the bias within our news organization. My boss automatically assumed that because I was pro-life, I was unable to be objective in my reporting. Recent polls clearly indicate that the vast majority of journalists and media professionals support legalized abortion, yet they think that they are the epitome of balance and objectivity. Survey after survey finds quite the opposite to be true.

Major recent news events have revealed the bias in the secular media. They include coverage of Mel Gibson's masterpiece, *The Passion of the Christ*, the drama surrounding the 2004 presidential elections, the 2005 starvation death of Terri Schiavo, coverage of the death of Pope John Paul II and election of Pope Benedict XVI, and the clamor surrounding the fictional movie *The Da Vinci Code*. Careless and irresponsible reporting, outright denial of truth, and lack of objectivity prevailed in the reporting of each event. As I reflect on the news coverage, I am reminded of a powerful quote I read in a trade magazine years ago when I was a starry-eyed journalism student. I had not been practicing my faith at the time, yet the words of Pope John Paul II astounded me. Speaking to reporters in New York during his 1979 visit to the United States, the pope said, "Be faithful to the truth and to its transmission, for truth endures, truth will not go away. Truth will not pass or change."[123] When I read the Pontiff's words, I thought to myself, "Wow! Someone in the church captured the essence of what the media are supposed to be."

My experience in the newsroom has shown me that, all too often, the truth is nowhere to be found. Personal agendas taint and twist news stories, right down to the way stories are written. I really believe that many reporters simply cannot handle the truth—and go out of their way to avoid it. CBS News could not handle the truth during the 2004 presidential election coverage, when it aired a story about President George W. Bush's service in the National Guard. Anchor Dan Rather, his producers, and others working on the "Memo-gate" story refused to admit that there were major red flags surrounding the source of the documents on which they based their story and the very documents themselves. As a result, CBS aired a flawed, pre-presidential 2004 election story. Retracting stories or correcting them later does little good. Once a story is aired, the damage has been done. Even if every single person is made aware of the mistake, credibility has already been lost and consumers are left doubting.

Dan Rather had long been known for his leftward leanings, and media critics were quick to point out that this was another example of his bias. Rather and CBS News dug in their heels and waited several weeks before issuing an apology. Months later, a panel released its report on the incident. CBS took pride in the fact that those who conducted the investigation claimed that it was not liberal bias that led to the problems, but a "myopic zeal," combined with newsroom cutbacks and pressure to produce major stories in less time. It is important to note, though, that CBS paid for the report. So it is very likely they were going to look for something positive on which to hang their hat. I have always wanted to ask the panelists hired by CBS about their conclusions. What in the world do they think leads to such "myopic zeal"? Usually, when we are passionate about a matter, we are blinded by our personal opinions and agendas, and determined to make a point. As I mentioned, Dan Rather's aversion to anything or anyone even slightly to the right of center is well known in the industry and well established by media activist groups.

When Rather was asked about the report's findings, he simply shrugged his shoulders and told the press, "I'll keep those things in mind." This type of arrogance is leading to a severe drop in the collective viewership of CBS, NBC, and ABC. This type of obvious bias also led to a huge imbalance in pre-election coverage. The only positive fallout from this egregious disregard of the truth was that it accelerated Dan Rather's retirement. The investigation into the handling of the story also led to pink slips for several other CBS employees, but the network ultimately came through with just a few bumps and bruises. As CBS struggled to revamp its image, they hired Katie Couric, not exactly a beacon of objectivity herself, to take over the *CBS Evening News*.

The Media Research Center showed the press went out of its way to favor Democrat John Kerry in the 2004 Presidential election, even to the point of doing more fact checking on President Bush's statements than on Kerry's.[124] Prior to the election, an interesting and condemning memo surfaced from ABC News political director Mark Halperin. He called upon his colleagues to hold the president more accountable, saying, "The current Bush attacks on Kerry involve distortions and taking things out of context in a way that goes beyond what Kerry has done." Halperin went on in the memo to explain that the general masses are basically just dumb Americans, people who are incapable of discerning fact from fiction. "It is up to Kerry to defend himself, of course, but as one of the few news organizations with the skill and strength to help voters evaluate what the candidates are saying and to serve the public interest, now is the time for all of us to step up and do what is right."[125] Evidently we need the brilliant minds of the media elite to set us straight. Since when does serving the public interest translate to limiting the investigative process to only one candidate? How can a reporter or editor do what is right when he or she is being told in writing to favor one candidate over the other by ignoring mistakes or exaggerations?

On November 1, 2004, just days before the election, the Center for Media and Public Affairs (CMPA) issued an alarming study about how the media coverage, especially the major broadcast news operations, blatantly favored John Kerry. CMPA said that Kerry received the most favorable network news coverage of any presidential candidate "since CMPA began tracking election news in 1988." The same report showed that coverage of the president was highly negative. Researchers based their findings on content analysis of news coverage from the three major television networks during the two-month period leading up to the election. John Kerry received fifty-eight percent positive coverage and forty-two percent negative, while George Bush received thirty-six percent positive coverage and sixty-four percent negative.[126]

In his best-selling book, *Arrogance: Rescuing America from the Media Elite,* former CBS correspondent Bernard Goldberg insists that today's journalists need to expand their horizons and realize that there are actually people who live outside of New York, Washington, D.C., and Los Angeles. Goldberg makes no bones about the fact that reporters in these cities who work at the big papers and networks are narrow-minded and provincial, even though they see themselves as sophisticated and worldly.

It's fascinating really how narrow and provincial is the world that supposedly sophisticated journalists have chosen to live in, how little they expose themselves to thoughts and opinions that challenge their liberal assumptions. Solutions? They're simple enough for any five-year-old to follow. First journalists need to stop sucking their thumbs and drop their blankets. It is time for them to broaden their horizons and open themselves up to all sorts of fun, new ideas.[127]

In addition to CBS, the *New York Times* and *USA Today,* two of the most widely-circulated and influential papers in the country, have had some recent trouble with accuracy. Each paper endured embarrassing plagiarism scandals involving one of its star reporters. Writers and editors from both national dailies tried warning management about signs they had been seeing, but it was too late. Both papers ended up printing apologies and retracting numerous falsified stories that made it into print, often on their front pages. The publications have also seen significant staff changes since, and have been forced to reevaluate their vetting and copyediting procedures.[128] In 1998, CNN was forced to admit that truth was lacking in what was dubbed the "Tailwind scandal." The cable network was forced to retract a story accusing the American military of using nerve gas to kill U.S. defectors in Laos during the Vietnam War.

Is it any wonder why media credibility is so low? According to a September 2004 Gallup poll, credibility in the news media hit a thirty-year low.[129] The poll found that just forty-four percent of Americans expressed confidence in the media's ability to report accurately.[130] This figure is a significant drop from 2003, when the media earned a fifty-four percent public-confidence rating. Gallup pollsters said the results were striking because confidence levels had only fluctuated between fifty-one and fifty-five percent during the six previous years. Gallup also found that forty-eight percent of Americans view the media as too liberal.[131]

The media increasingly chooses to ignore the truth and invent its own truths, especially where moral issues are concerned.[132] A blatant example was the horrible starvation death of Terri Schiavo. In early 2005, Pinellas County, Florida became the site of a media circus. Many listeners who called my radio program had no idea that Terri's husband Michael was actually her estranged husband. While raising another family with another woman, Michael fought vehemently, under the guise that he wanted to carry out Terri's wishes, to have her feeding tube removed. Years earlier, before the heart attack that left her brain dead, Terri allegedly made a comment to Michael about never wanting "to live like that," referring to a television program about a person on life support. The secular media failed to objectively report Michael's living arrangement during the controversy over Terri's feeding tube. Instead, they portrayed him as a loving husband whose only interest was his wife's cause. How could someone who has obviously moved on in his life—to the point of raising another family with his girlfriend—have Terri's best interests in mind?

The tragic case of Terri Schiavo is an instructive example of how the media invents the truth. Why didn't reporters consult their legal experts, or Michael Schiavo himself, about the obvious conflict of interest? If Mr. Schiavo loved and cared for his wife so much, then why wouldn't he stay by her side instead of starting another family while he was still married to Terri? Since when does a mere statement someone makes about something they supposedly saw on a television show become the legally-binding statement that determines their fate? What about those allegations of past abuse on the part of Schiavo? Why did Schiavo insist that his wife be cremated? These are just a few of the questions that a thoughtful, balanced press should have raised again and again.

The media also failed to report the background of Schiavo's attorney, George Felos, who is an ardent advocate of euthanasia. Felos has written and spoken extensively about the topic. However, we heard very little about Felos during the on-going court battles. Most of the stories we did see and hear were released after Terri's death. The media and other euthanasia advocates allowed Felos to repeatedly claim that the fight for Terri's life was all part of some right-wing religious conspiracy. He cleverly played the religion card against Terri's advocates to keep the spotlight off his own "spiritual" agenda. Fox News and Catholic and Protestant press organizations were the only outlets that gave the issue of "right to life" plausible coverage. Mainstream media concentrated instead on "the right to die." It is tragic that the vast majority of Americans were not able to hear about the depth and breadth of Catholic teaching on life issues as Terri Schiavo was slowing being killed.

One of the most egregious examples of how the media was simply inventing its own truth in the Schiavo case centered on the issue of cremation. During a live interview on my radio program, Terri's father, Robert Schindler, said he suspected that Michael Schiavo insisted on cremating Terri because Michael was worried about what an autopsy might uncover. Then, just days before Terri died, it appeared, from media accounts, that Michael had a sudden change of heart and was willingly going to allow an autopsy. In a March 30, 2005 story in the *St. Petersburg Times* (one of the few papers to explain what really happened with the autopsy), George Felos attempted to again paint his client as hero. "He believes it is important to have the public know the full and massive extent of the damage to Mrs. Schiavo's brain," Felos said.[133] However, the real reason for the change of heart was revealed in the article. It had nothing to do with Michael Schiavo's so-called good intentions. It was a matter of Florida law. According to Florida statute 406.11, the state requires an autopsy for someone who dies in unusual circumstances. The law also requires the medical examiner's involvement when a body is cremated. Felos had successfully reeled the media in on another PR stunt—hook, line, and sinker.

The Media Research Center (MRC) carefully studied bias in the news coverage of the Schiavo case. It found that the three major broadcast network evening newscasts had slanted coverage in favor of Michael Schiavo. Examining all thirty-one evening news stories broadcast from March 17, 2005, the day before Terri's feeding tube was removed, to March 21, fifty-nine percent of the sound bites criticized lawmakers for fighting to bring the case to a federal court.[134]

According to the MRC, not one network story during this period was skeptical of Michael Schiavo.[135]

A priest friend of mine says that the devil strikes first, but God always has the last word. This was evident in the case of Terri Schiavo. As Terri's feeding tube was being removed, Pope John Paul II was having a feeding tube inserted. The mainstream media was trying to justify the notion that life is dispensable and we should be able to end it whenever and however we choose. During the final days of the pope's life, though, God showed us that every life is precious and that great understanding and good can come from suffering.

Coverage of the pope's death was generally positive, according to the MRC. Every major network and newspaper, along with hordes of still photographers, captured the sounds, sights, and statements of the millions of pilgrims who flocked to Rome to pay their respects. The reporters interviewed people from the four corners of the globe, many of whom told moving stories about their love for the pope. They gave witness to the effect of Christ in their lives as they explained their willingness to wait in lines for up to eighteen hours to get a brief glimpse of the Holy Father's body as it lay in state at St. Peter's. The solemn funeral Mass was beamed to television sets around the world. Even the Arab TV network carried the broadcast. The Catholic news agency ZENIT said John Paul II's death attracted an unprecedented level of interest from media around the world.[136] Among his other achievements, John Paul was acknowledged for his triumphant opposition to communism. The Global Language Monitor (GBL), which tracks and analyzes media coverage, reported twelve million Internet citations and more than one hundred thousand stories in media outlets around the world on the day of his funeral which led to GBL putting the death of John Paul at the top of its list of Global Media Stories of 2005.[137] The coverage exceeded the media attention given to other major world events, including the terrorist attacks of September 11, 2001, the Southeast Asian tsunami, the death of president Ronald Reagan, and even the death of Princess Diana. ZENIT reported a noticeable increase of hits to Catholic Internet sites, with a recorded 118 percent jump in market share of on-line visits for the week ending April 9, 2005. Pope John Paul II's passing also prompted a deluge of Internet searches, which were up over three thousand percent in the days following his death.[138] This period of mourning was also a time for the faithful to celebrate, because one of their own was actually being portrayed properly.

However, within a week of John Paul's funeral, the breath of the liberal vipers could be felt. Truth often hurts, and the media, especially in America, could not handle it. Inconsistencies in coverage of the pope and his death began to emerge. In their 2005 report, *The Life of Pope John Paul II: Shepherd of Souls or Antiquated Authoritarian?,* the

Media Research Center exposed the many inconsistencies in news coverage of the pope. MRC analysts quoted stories from *Newsweek*, the AP, the *Washington Post*, ABC, and other outlets that repeatedly showed reporter bias toward Catholic moral teachings. Issues such as contraception, abortion, and female priests began to dominate stories. As MRC President Brent Bozell explained, the media just does not understand that Catholic teaching, including the choosing of a new pope, is not decided by democratic vote. "The major media consistently comment on which direction the world should take, and reporters are doing the same with the Catholic Church," Bozell said. "They consistently lobbied the pope to invent a more convenient Church that defines holiness down for its members."[139]

As the world's cardinals gathered in Rome to elect the new pope, the media began quoting polls that allegedly revealed an interest among American Catholics for a more liberal pontiff, one who would be softer on issues such as same-sex marriage, abortion, euthanasia, women's ordination, contraception, and premarital sex. According to one CBS News report, "many Catholics found nothing to celebrate."[140] Who were these "many" Catholics? CBS News or its pollsters certainly did not ask me, my friends, or my radio listeners, who love the Church and believe she speaks with the authority of Christ on these moral matters, for our comments. Before embracing my faith in recent years, I professed myself to be a Catholic, even if I graced the doors of a church only at Christmas and Easter or for an occasional wedding or funeral. Intellectually, though, I knew I was out to lunch on the theology behind my faith; I was short on opinions about what the Church taught. So it is easy for me to understand the mindset of many "cultural" Catholics, and I wonder what percentage of the people who were allegedly polled or questioned actually represented *practicing* Catholics. How many who profess the Catholic faith really understand the Church's teachings? How many have even a working knowledge of the *Catechism* or have read apologetics materials which explain and defend the logic of Catholic teachings? I do not raise these questions in condemnation. I raise them because of my personal experience as a casual Catholic. Consider this analogy. If a Gallup pollster were to call me and ask my opinion on NASA, the government would be wise to ignore my answer when making decisions about the future of space shuttles. In much the same way, little credence should be placed on the surveys of semi-informed Catholics.

Media coverage of the election of Pope Benedict XVI also became an interesting spectator sport for Catholic pundits. Unlike the praise bestowed upon John Paul II in the first few days following his death, the media attacked Pope Benedict right out of the gate. Reporters covering the election of the 265th Pope were in shock that the Church would choose someone they deemed a "hard-line conservative," "the enforcer," and "God's rottweiler." The mainstream press insists the Church is "out of touch."

Several practicing Catholic journalists, who, like me, have worked in the secular media, have begun to express their frustrations with the media's coverage of the Church. Former Detroit newswoman Vanessa Denha-Garmo worked for years as a successful radio reporter and anchorwoman. She now serves as a public relations consultant and editor-in-chief of the *Chaldean News*, a monthly Michigan newspaper. As Denha-Garmo notes:

> In terms of faith, Catholicism is not popular with the mainstream media. Yes, the media reported on the pope extensively, which was refreshing, but when it comes to Catholic issues on a regular basis, they ignore the Church. You don't see the mainstream media covering the negative health effects an abortion has on a woman's body, let alone that it is killing another human being.[141]

The liberal bias against Benedict reached new lows when more than a few papers prematurely ran sizable headlines about Benedict's early association with the Hitler's Youth movement. What they didn't highlight was that joining the movement was compulsory and that he disassociated himself with the fascist movement as soon as he was able. Imagine the backlash if newspapers ran similar slanders against Muslim leaders. There would be public protest and certain firings, not to mention possible death threats. Attacks on Catholicism, though, are fair game.

Blatant anti-Catholic bias also reared its ugly head in countless instances during the release of *The Da Vinci Code* in 2006. The Media Research Center again pointed out how the news media, prior to the film's debut at the celebrated Cannes Film Festival, did what it could to discredit the Catholic Church. The liberal media encouraged and promoted the baseless and utterly ridiculous ideas of *Da Vinci Code* author Dan Brown. The press embraced Brown, director Ron Howard, and Tom Hanks, while Mel Gibson and Jim Caviezel were insulted and shunned by Hollywood during the release of *The Passion of the Christ.* Why was Gibson attacked for his portrayal of Jesus while Ron Howard was not? (Note: This was two years before Gibson's widely-reported, anti-Semitic comments.) The answer is obvious to me. The media did not like the accurate traditional Jesus who condemned sin, suffered and died for us, and rose from the dead. They wanted no part of a savior who changes lives through a call to conversion. Instead, as the Media Research Center pointed out, they jumped at the opportunity to promote an earthly savior who had a girlfriend and sired a child. In its special report, *The Trashing of the Christ,* the MRC showed that *The Da Vinci Code* received more of a publicity push from the networks than *The Passion of the Christ.* Before its May 19, 2005 release, *The Da Vinci Code* racked up ninety-nine segments on the networks compared to only sixty-six prior to the release of *The Passion.*[142] The MRC cited that most of the pre-release coverage for *The Da Vinci Code* was very positive. This, of course, was definitely not the case with *The Passion.* Mel Gibson's film, according to the MRC, was actually treated "as a social problem and the biggest television anti-Semitism story of that year. Meanwhile, *The Da Vinci Code* was presented, more often than not, as intriguing theory rather than something that was seriously offensive to Christians."[143] The MRC stated that nearly all of the sixty-six reports on the major networks concerning *The Passion* dealt with complaints about the movie while only twenty-seven of the ninety-nine segments on *The Da Vinci Code* concentrated on complaints from Christians.[144]

Once the movie hit the theatres, a majority of film critics in the European and American press, who panned the film, referred to it as *"Duh Vinci," "Dull Vinci,"* and *"The Da Vinci Dud."* However, most of the reviews focused on the production and acting and not the religious references. The reviewers did not seem too upset at the shots taken at Christ, the Catholic Church, or by extension, nearly two billion Christians around the world. They were more upset about Tom Hanks' bad hair and his lackluster portrayal of Professor Robert Langdon than the slanderous lies about Jesus and the Church. Despite the bad reviews, *The Da Vinci Code* made several hundred million dollars, becoming one of the most successful films in Hollywood history. The MRC report concluded that the media's obsessive reporting on the movie had much to do with the film's financial windfall. Promotions for *The Da Vinci Code* encouraged moviegoers to "seek the truth," but the media wanted little part of the actual truth about Christ and the Catholic Church.

I am often asked why the media is so biased and sympathetic toward liberal causes. The answer is really very simple. The majority of people who work in the media are liberal. For this reason, pro-life groups are referred to as "anti-choice" and anti-life groups are referred to as "pro-choice." This is also the reason why most of the happy people on television are sexually permissive and most of the religious people are portrayed as repressive, uptight, and nerdy.

One of the most well known studies on liberal media bias was conducted in 1981. The Lichter and Rothman survey of 240 journalists at top national media outlets, both print and broadcast, revealed how top reporters openly described themselves as liberal, with fifty-four percent admitting they were "left of center."[145] In the mid-1980s, the *Los Angeles Times* conducted its own survey of reporters around the country and obtained similar results. Fifty-five percent of the media polled called themselves liberal, eighty-two percent said they supported legalized abortion, sixty-seven percent opposed prayer in public schools, and seventy-eight percent supported stricter handgun control.[146] Since then, the number of journalists who readily identify themselves as liberal, has increased.

In 1996, a Freedom Forum report of Washington media elites found that sixty-one percent identified themselves as liberal.[147] The figures speak for themselves, leaving little doubt as to why the media is so blatantly anti-Christian. In his 2003 message at World Communication Day, Pope John Paul II warned of the damaging effects from the media's approach to religion.

> In fact the media often do render courageous service to the truth; but sometimes they function as agents of propaganda and misinformation in the service of narrow interests, national, ethnic, racial, and religious prejudices, material greed, and false ideologies of various kids. It is imperative that the pressures brought to bear on the media to err in such ways be resisted first of all by the men and women of the media themselves but also by the Church and other concerned groups.[148]

Journalists like to call themselves "objective," but any journalism professor worth his or her salt will tell you that there is no such thing as complete objectivity. We all bring our life experiences to any given story. It is human nature to surround ourselves with like-minded people. That said, journalists are still called to leave personal opinions on the editing floor. It is the job of journalists to report all sides of a story. Any newsperson that claims to be totally objective is simply not being honest about himself or the business. When one of my television producers started her family, the station suddenly began airing stories on childcare and child health issues. The producer's world had opened up and she saw a niche in need of media attention.

When another news staffer purchased his first home, the station began covering stories about home improvement. Subjectivity on news coverage is acceptable to a degree. Realistically, complete objectivity is almost impossible to attain, but striving for it is not impossible.

Be aware, too, that the news business is run *as a business*. Most major media outlets are owned by publicly-traded companies, which are driven by making money. Although I still believe liberal bias was a major factor in the CBS "Memo-gate" scandal, I can easily see how the producers were pushed to air a story before they had time to check and recheck their sources, facts, and documentation. The network wasn't thinking of accuracy; it was thinking of ratings. Today's editors, reporters, and writers are under substantial pressure to produce more content at less cost. An alarming report released in March 2005 by the Poynter Institute for Media Studies showed just how much of an uphill battle some news operations face to not only get the job done, but also to get it done right. *Out of Balance: Poynter Survey Reveals Journalists' Pressure Points* showed that among its 750 respondents, sixty-five percent always work more than forty hours a week, forty-six percent did not take all their vacation time, and sixty-seven percent saw staff reductions over the past two years. The survey also found that forty-seven percent have seriously considered leaving journalism.[149]

Sensationalism, driven by the need for high ratings, is another major factor in today's news coverage. Stations who secure bigger ratings can increase their advertising rates and thus their profits. I saw this play out more frequently in my last few years as a television news reporter. On one particular occasion I was sent to cover a Mothers against Drunk Driving (MADD) press conference at a local mall. The main speaker was a father who had lost his teenage daughter in a horrible accident a year earlier. His daughter and her friends had not been drinking, and they had followed all the rules, including wearing seatbelts. The oncoming driver, however, did not follow the rules. After running a stop sign, she hit the teens' car head-on. The grieving father gave a very moving statement about why he had joined MADD. After the press conference, I asked him a few more questions. I felt I had a very powerful piece to share that would help raise consciousness among our viewers. The station, however, had other ideas. I was expected to turn around a live report for the next newscast, but I quickly discovered that my bosses were not interested in the father's statement or his insightful answers to my follow-up questions. I almost dropped the phone when I heard my producer's instructions: "Forget the video. We want you to take him back to the scene of the accident and do a live shot there. It will make for great emotion and you could probably get him to cry on camera." I was appalled. Dragging the poor man back to the scene had nothing to do with getting the truth out about the dangers of drunk driving. It had everything to do with ratings and sensationalism. I argued with the powers that be and eventually the story was done my way. I can remember going home that day feeling drained, frustrated, and disillusioned.

On another occasion, I was working the late shift and was asked to follow up on another crash involving some local high-school students. The young driver had tried to get across the railroad tracks to beat an oncoming train, but he didn't make it. He and all of his passengers were killed. I was assigned to capture an interview with the victim's family at their home. Producers wanted footage of the family pouring their hearts out. I told my cameraman that we would just drive to the area, wait a little while, and then head back to the station to rework the video and the sound gathered earlier in the day. There was no reason to put the family through more misery. He agreed. We had to go to the neighborhood, since our news vehicles were equipped with tracking systems. We planned to just hide out for a while and then go back to the station, but it is pretty hard to be inconspicuous in a television news truck. Within seconds of turning onto the street, a man came out of his house screaming and yelling at us, demanding that we leave his family alone. I was embarrassed and didn't blame him one bit. I thought about rolling down the window to explain our intentions, but instead I decided we should simply leave immediately, and we did. Later that night, I sat in the news van asking myself, "Is this what the business has come to?" I was sick to my stomach. When I got back to the newsroom, my heart sank even further as I glanced at the statement from John Paul II, as I had so many times over the years. The bold headline atop it read, "Something Worthy of Your Best Years." The pope wrote:

> If your reporting does not always command the attention you would desire, or if it does not always conclude with the success you would wish, do not grow discouraged. Be faithful to the truth and to its transmission for truth endures, truth will not go away. Truth will not pass or change. And I say to you—take it as my parting words to you— that the service of truth, the service of humanity through the medium of truth is something worthy of your best years, your finest talents, your most dedicated efforts.[150]

Despite the media's attempt to distort the truth to advance a liberal agenda, twist the facts to make stories more appealing, and hype the news in an attempt to hike ratings, John Paul II is correct—"Truth will not pass or change."

The truth is eventually revealed through God's intervention and perfect timing. A case in point: look at what happened in January of 2007 with the latest breakthrough on stem-cell research. It took seven years for the research to get published, but scientists report they are now able to successfully retrieve and manipulate stem cells found in amniotic fluid and that the cells have great potential similar to embryonic stem cells. The story broke the same week the U.S. Congress was debating a measure to force taxpayers to support government funding of embryonic stem-cell research. This is one of those hot-button issues where the secular press often only tells half the story, portraying the Catholic Church and others as being against stem-cell research. (In truth, the Church supports adult stem-cell research, which does not involve the taking of human life as does stem-cell research using human embryos.) The media also fail to report the dangers and the complications that come with tampering with human embryos for research, including the risks or growth of tumors. In addition, not one person has ever been helped by embryonic stem-cell research (not that this would justify such research), while some seventy-two different diseases or conditions have been treated or can benefit from non-embryonic stem-cell research. Sometimes news outlets even avoid talking about the destruction of human embryos. That's why it is a certain sign of hope that the secular press not only covered the story but also finally started to include some of the negative aspects of embryonic stem-cell research.

For example, ABC News reported that "these cells can be gathered without hurting the mother or the fetus and would prove much less controversial than research done with embryos."[151] The *Los Angeles Times* said the research showed "great promise" and that it "sidesteps the hurdles facing embryonic stem-cell research, which has been stymied by moral objections to the destruction of embryos that occur when the cells are harvested."[152] As with the series in the

Detroit News, this issue represents a teachable moment for Catholics. Joe Cella, president of the Catholic lay organization, Fidelis, says it is similar to the moment in the mid-1990s when the grisly act of partial-birth abortion was first exposed.

Now seven out of ten Americans oppose partial birth abortion. The reason for this shift is not because of the media, but because the pro-life movement worked hard to educate the public. The amniotic stem cell research breakthrough presents a tremendous opportunity for the pro-life movement to squelch many of the misconceptions as the stem cell debate continues.[153]

We simply have to engage the media and the culture to make sure that the truth is proclaimed. How do we do this? By being *proactive* instead of merely *reactive* when it comes to issues that concern the faithful, especially life issues; by writing concise letters to the editor, void of *ad hominem* attacks and anger; by being persistent in one's efforts, not expecting the media to respond after a single phone call or press release; and by building relationships with local and national media by providing them with solid resources to consult and experts to interview. As Blessed Teresa of Calcutta has said, "God doesn't expect us to be successful, only faithful." By making an effort to witness the truth to the media, you will not only be faithful—you may even be successful. You might just make a difference in the news climate of your local newspaper, television station, or even on the media at large.

MAKING A DIFFERENCE IN THE NEWS MEDIA

Action Items

1. Pray for the secular media.
2. Support and subscribe to Catholic news media outlets.
3. Monitor local news and public-affairs programming to see if stories are being covered fairly and accurately.
4. Build relationships with members of the local media.
5. Be willing to meet with members of the local media, especially news managers and newspaper editorial boards.
6. Be proactive with the press by offering sources and story ideas.
7. Write letters to the editor.
8. Provide positive as well as negative feedback on news coverage.
9. When filing a complaint, give the reporter a chance to respond and explain.
10. Approach the media in a Christ-like manner. Practice the approach, "Always be ready to give a defense for the hope that is within you but do it with gentleness and reverence" (1 Peter 3:15).

CHAPTER 14

The Stranger in Your Home

Circa 1950, a young father who was intrigued with the personality of a stranger he had just met invited the stranger home. Immediately upon introduction, this newcomer also fascinated the man's wife and children. The family instantly became attached and invited the stranger to stay for good. The visitor was the family storyteller, who kept everyone spellbound for hours on end with adventures, mysteries, and humorous episodes. None of the children questioned the stranger's place in the family. As they grew and matured, the children turned to the stranger for answers about politics, history, and science. Ah, he was a most welcomed guest, so much so that when the stranger began to talk too much, and even about taboo topics like sex and violence, no one in the family asked him to leave. No one seemed to mind when the stranger began using foul language or advocated the use of alcohol and tobacco. In later years the stranger had openly begun to discuss and celebrate homosexuality, adultery, and premarital sex. He glamorized the occult. He elevated the status of celebrities and promoted vices like vanity, indulgence, and greed.

Today, more than fifty years later, the father is a very old man. His children have moved out and started their own families, yet the stranger still lives in the man's home. The stranger occupies the same corner of the den that he has since he was invited into the home. The stranger's name is television, and despite all the offenses this stranger has committed against the family, the adult children have invited him into their homes as well.

The preceding analogy, likening television to a stranger, has been circulating on the Internet in recent years. It eloquently describes our current state of affairs. Tens of millions of American families have invited this stranger into their homes over the past five or six decades, and they invited the strangers' offspring, too: cable TV, pay-per-view, DVDs, and video games that are even bolder than the original stranger. They show explicit sex, speak vilely about the human person, especially women, and push the limits of immorality to heights never before imagined.

According to the National Institute on Media and the Family, children spend almost as much time using media as most adults do working.[154] The ramifications of this sordid diet are truly incalculable. The average American youth watches at least twenty-five hours of television each week. Add to that time spent with other media outlets like the Internet, cell phones, iPods, radio, magazines, and video games, and they likely rack up more overtime in one week than most adults do in a month. At the very least, our youth spend more than a quarter of their very existence each week with some form of isolated media.

The story of the stranger played out in my home and very likely yours, too. What would happen if the stranger were an actual person? I bet his provocative nature and arrogance would land him out on the street before long. Very few of us would tolerate a real stranger's attack on our children or willingly allow another to undermine our Christian beliefs. However, television and other media outlets do this every day. Why do we allow our children to get information from anybody and everybody on important topics like human sexuality and relationships? When we are not vigilant about what our families watch on TV, we allow the stranger to set precedence and influence our lives.

According to the Kaiser Family Foundation, parents admit that it would be difficult to function without televisions in their home.[155] Television offers parents a bit of relief, an opportunity to check off their "to do" lists, or a small break from the often raucous squabbling among siblings. How many of us, though, actually pay attention to what is being watched in the other room? I am not standing in judgment, but simply sounding an alarm that the house is on fire. We have to be prepared and carry our extinguishers at all times. The TV can be as beneficial to us as it is harmful, but we need to take charge and call the shots. That is, we need to know which programs are good and which are potential hazards.

Parents who spend their hard-earned cash on Catholic or other private Christian schools, but who are not adamant about their children's media habits, could very well be wasting their money, especially given the anti-Christian messages that are beamed into our homes through a variety of sources each day. These messages undermine the very moral lessons children are learning in schools and at the dinner table.

A plethora of media messages overtly and covertly challenges the Catholic faith. Take Madonna for example. In the summer of 2006, she opened her music tour in Los Angeles. Curiously titled "Confessions," the controversial tour was widely discussed in the media. Creating controversy has always been Madonna's marketing ploy. Her show was jam-packed with oral-sex jokes and liberal political statements. Most offensive, though, was the opening of her show, where she appeared hanging from a cross wearing a crown of thorns. William Donahue, president of the Catholic League for Religious and Civil Rights, thought there was a glimmer of hope for the pop star a few years back, when she embraced Kabbalah, a form of Jewish mysticism. Donahue had hoped that after twenty years of sacrilege, Madonna would begin to show respect for religion, but, alas, this was not the case.

> It stands to reason that a woman whose faith is so important to her that she drags her rabbi to her concerts would not want to mock the faith of others. But I guess you can't teach old pop stars new tricks. Madonna has been spicing up her act with misappropriated Christian imagery for a long time now. Perhaps she can't arouse any more interest in her work without it. Poor Madonna keeps trying to shock. But all she succeeds in doing is coming across as a boring bigot. Do us a favor, Madge, and stick to singing and dancing. Knock off the Christ-bashing. It's just pathetic.[156]

While Madonna's antics may fail to shock adults who are accustomed to her routine, she still has thousands of adoring young fans who flock to her concerts, buy her music, watch her on MTV, and log onto her website. In a sense, we contribute to the success of Madonna and her cronies when we do not actively protest their actions.

While Madonna was up to her clever image marketing tricks, the real Madonna, the Blessed Mother, was being mocked, defiled, and insulted along with Pope Benedict during a Christmas season episode of the popular Comedy Central show *South Park*. The show's creators thought it would be fun to center a December 2005 episode on a bleeding Virgin Mary statue. Out of respect for the Mother of God, I will spare the details here, but the cable station went as far as to air the episode on the eve of the Immaculate Conception, the feast day which celebrates the Catholic dogma that Mary was sinless from the first moment of her conception. After numerous complaints, Comedy Central pulled re-runs of the *Bloody Mary* episode, but how much damage had already been done?

These are but a few of the blatant examples of how the stranger has overtaken our homes, undermining parental authority and the Gospel values we try to instill. We know we cannot rely on the ratings systems which are self-imposed by each medium. As far as tools like the V-chip, a parental-control device installed in all new television sets since 2000, the Kaiser Foundation has found that many parents have little understanding of the television ratings system and only fifteen percent use the V-Chip.[157] This is why we must limit the time our children spend with the media and restrict certain programs and activities.

A national survey by Public Agenda in 2002 showed that parents felt they were "hit and miss" in terms of teaching values. In fact, many had considered themselves failures in the values department, but they did recognize television's downward trend of program content. Almost ninety percent implicated television as the biggest hurdle in their efforts to teach their children.[158]

If there is any good news to report, it is that the current state of media degradation has prompted interest and action from all sides of the religious and political spectrums. So much so that a new law, the Broadcast Decency Enforcement Act of 2005, was approved by Congress by an overwhelming bipartisan margin and signed by President George W. Bush. The measure increased tenfold the amount broadcasters can be fined for airing indecent material, from $32,500 to $325,000 per violation. President Bush said he signed the measure because the government "has a responsibility to help strengthen families and the law would make television and radio more family-friendly by allowing the government agency that oversees broadcasters to impose stiffer fines."[159] This is great news for those of us who are anxious to see a turn in the morally corrupt tide, including the hundreds of thousands who filed complaints against broadcasters in the first part of 2005. More than 275,000 complaints about obscene and indecent material on the radio and television were filed with the FCC in the first four months of 2005, compared to a mere 44,000 complaints filed in the last quarter of 2004.

As Christians we are called to show kindness to strangers, but allowing them to move in and overrun our homes and corrupt our values is going a bit too far. Media gadgetry clutters our homes, our daily lives, and our minds, creating so much noise that our common sense is drowned and there is little room for reflection and for God. However, all is not lost. With God everything is possible.

CHAPTER 15

Becoming a Media-Savvy Family

"I don't worry about TV because we don't have one anymore in our home. I threw it our years ago and never looked back. So I don't have to worry about the media impacting me or my family." A mom shared this with me at one of my seminars a few years ago. Although some may see this as a proper response to the state of affairs, I actually do not. Throwing the television (or radio or the computer) out the window is to hand the media over to the evil one. Unless this woman and her children are sequestered 24/7 or live underground, the media most definitely will impact them once they come up for light. Even those who try to protect themselves as best they can in the home can't escape the noise outside the home. Televisions, computers, cell phones, billboards, and blaring radios are in retail stores, restaurants, airports, and cars. The noise is everywhere. We need a different approach to control the media's influence in our lives.

My cousin, Jean, is a great example of what it means to be truly media savvy. A middle-aged mother of four, Jean teaches at a Catholic school in Michigan and knows all too well how the media can affect young people. She says she started setting ground rules when her kids were young, so today they know their boundaries pretty well. One time she and her family were so disturbed by some inappropriate messages on one of their favorite programs that they sat down and wrote a letter together to the network as a family. She later explained to me that not only did she give her kids a great lesson in media activism, but the situation gave her an opportunity to reinforce a lesson on what is and is not appropriate viewing. She was able to reinforce the family's values.

To completely detach our families from major media is to throw the baby out with the bath water. As I pointed out previously, even the late Pope John Paul II saw value in the media and an opportunity there to spread the Good News. The pope said, "If it doesn't happen on television, it doesn't happen."[160] Without television, the world might not have come to know John Paul in the manner in which it did. The pope stressed the importance of making media usage a family activity that includes and involves parents. Excellent programming can be found on EWTN, the Hallmark and Discovery Channels, and on PBS, just to name a few. Becoming a media-savvy Catholic means finding the good content in the various media outlets and learning to control the amount of time spent with it. Feed your family intellectually and spiritually by making wholesome media choices and evangelize by responding to bad content through letter writing and phone calls.

Being an activist on behalf of the truth is also an act of charity toward society.

Consider a smoking analogy. Those of us who choose not to smoke live in smoke-free homes. Our immediate environments are healthy. Until recently, this was not the case when we went out in public. Once upon a time, cigarette smoke was virtually unavoidable; it was everywhere. This changed over time because we demanded change. We stood up for our right to enjoy a meal in a public restaurant without having to deal with the annoyance of cigarette smoke blowing from the table next to us. The majority of us detested smoky environments. So, change occurred. We made it happen and we can make it happen in the media, too. Just like the media industry, the tobacco industry is big business, yet it was forced to bow to public pressure.

The first step to creating a wave of change requires cleaning up our habits at home. From there, we should make our voices heard to management at the individual media outlets and to their advertisers. We can do this through letter writing, e-mails, phone calls, and petition drives. Just as important as complaint letters are our letters of praise for programming we find favorable, and also our suggestions. As evidenced by the stiffer FCC fines for broadcast indecency, public pressure does prompt change. Measures such as stiffer fines for indecency will force the media to be more responsible, as will a word or two from their sponsors. In addition to the action items that follow each of the media chapters, consult *Your Family Media Guide* at the end of this book for information on how to contact the major media outlets in the United States.

Remember—it is never too late to set ground rules at home. Friends of mine created plastic laminated cards that serve as television and video game "allowance cards." Every Friday, the two older children, ages seven and nine, are given six-hours' worth of TV cards and three-hours' worth of video cards that can be cashed in during the following week. Their parents explain that watching television and playing video games is not a right but a privilege. The kids are also warned that they can lose allowance cards if they get out of line or fail to cooperate in any serious way throughout the week. Likewise, they can earn extra allowance if they go above and beyond the call of duty in a special way during the week.

Another family I know of simply places time limits on electronics. When the children behave well, they are rewarded with an extra half hour of television or video-game privileges. Likewise, failure to comply with ground rules, can result in confiscation of electronic devices, including cell phones, iPods, and the teenagers' graphing calculators, which are also equipped with video games. The children understand that if mom or dad is forced to confiscate a calculator they will have to suffer the consequences at school.

A media-savvy parent explains the differences between appropriate and inappropriate television and radio programs, music, music videos, games, movies and websites. They also set parameters in the home and stick to them. It is important that children see consistency in their parents' directives, and it is likely that they will carry out those directives themselves, as they get older. Also, explaining the reasons behind the decisions instead of simply saying no provides a mutual understanding. That does not mean children will always agree with parental reasoning, but they will understand and ultimately respect it. When possible, watch television with children. The activity can help spark good family discussions

One Voice Can Make a Difference
(But 100,000 Voices Are Better)

One person with a vision has started many an initiative. There are so many things we can do as individuals to turn back the tide. We can start a petition drive, set up a website to protest a show, boycott advertisers, write letters to public officials. We never fully know what spark can start a raging fire. Our voices can be attached to thousands of others by joining an activist movement. One of the best is the Parents Television Council (PTC). The PTC's website, www.parentstv.org, offers a wealth of information. Any study ever done on media influence as well as the latest array of offenses to faith and family values can be found at the site. It also contains sample e-mails and letters, and a convenient list of the names of network executives and their advertisers. This site has it all, including a long list of success stories of grassroots initiatives.

The American Family Association (www.afa.net) and the National Coalition for the Protection of Children and Families (www.nationalcoalition.org) are two other favorites of mine. These groups run campaigns challenging all forms of media and are experts at countering the plague of pornography. For those who are fed up with all the sleazy commercials and ads on television or in print, the American Family Association (AFA) has two separate websites, www.OneMillionMoms.com and www.OneMillionDads.com. Each offers helpful suggestions on speaking out. The AFA has been successful in getting major corporations to pay attention to what kind of programs the companies are sponsoring. It was the AFA that alerted the public to problems with NBC's *The Book of Daniel*, a prime-time show that offended millions by featuring an Episcopalian priest as a drug addict, his bishop as a drunk, and a Catholic priest as a friend to organized crime. The AFA launched a grassroots effort to put pressure on advertisers, and it worked. Almost every advertiser on the show cancelled their sponsorships, and the program was yanked off the air after just a few weeks. Be sure to sign up for the free newsletters that most of these groups distribute. They are a great way to stay informed.

The Media Research Center's website, www. MediaResearch.org, is an excellent source on media bias and sensationalism. A word to the wise, though—be sure to check your blood pressure before logging on, as you may be shocked by the countless examples of shear media craziness. This site also offers suggestions on how to contact major media outlets.

Contacting *local* media representatives is also effective in exacting change. However, before complaining about an inaccuracy in a report, give the reporter a chance to explain himself. Someone other than the reporter or anchor often has the final word on what makes the cut. On countless occasions, I would leave a story with a producer for the eleven o'clock news only to kick my feet up at home that night and watch a significantly changed final product. Therefore, give a reporter a day or two to reply to a phone call or an e-mail. Most reporters spend little time in the office and are very busy trying to meet deadlines. After a few days, contact the reporter's supervisor, which is usually a bureau chief, news editor, or news director. When you do make contact with someone, be gentle, calm, and clear. Ask the person if he or she is on deadline. In many cases they are, and the courtesy of your question will likely guarantee a return call. Deadlines are not difficult to figure out. Newspaper deadlines vary depending upon whether the publication is a morning or evening paper. Weeklies usually have a soft deadline of thirty-six hours prior to production. So if a paper comes out on Saturdays, it is best to avoid calling on Thursday or Friday. Television newsrooms are most hectic in the hour before a newscast. Therefore, it is best to attempt to make contact several hours before a broadcast or immediately following a broadcast.

The Best Defense Is a Good Offense

Being *proactive* instead of *reactive* is an approach that we should adopt. Be assured that liberal activists groups proactively contact the media to push their agendas. We Christians need to do the same. We need to tell producers and editors about our celebrations, beliefs, and hopes. In other words, do not just contact the media to complain but also to introduce story ideas. So many deserving activities go unnoticed. It is up to us to do our own PR. Do you represent an active lay committee that conducts great programs at your church? Are you involved in a pro-life group? Do you lead a Christian youth ministry that is impacting the lives of young people or making a difference in the community? If so, establish relationships with reporters, producers, and editors so you can share your stories and ideas. In many ways, it's a numbers game. The more stories a particular group feeds the media, the more coverage they will get. Consistently good stories will also secure coverage, but do not expect constant coverage, and never give up. Don't be surprised if the media contacts you make begin to come to you on occasion for a sound bite.

Due to major events in the Catholic Church, an array of new Catholic spokespeople have found themselves in the national spotlight. That was no accident. It was actually the fruit of some media-savvy planning and good old-fashioned hard work on the part of Catholic marketing and public relations experts. These lay leaders decided to seize the moment when it became clear that Pope John Paul II was near death. Knowing that the media would be in need of Catholic spokespeople, yet concerned that the media would turn to voices that dissented from Catholic teaching, the Maximus Media Group ventured into foreign territory. The result was beyond the expectations of their small but feisty staff. In the weeks surrounding the death of Pope John Paul II and election of Benedict XVI, Maximus placed dozens of respected Catholic voices on more than two hundred national media interviews, including *Larry King Live, Good Morning America, Hannity and Colmes,* and *At Large with Geraldo Rivera.* It was a glorious moment for the Church. Maximus Media now employs a team of full-time public relations and marketing specialists who work daily to get faithful Catholic voices in the national and local media.

Supporting Catholic Media

Another great way to become media savvy and proactive regarding the faith is to lend your financial support to Christian media outlets, especially to those that do not have the advertising budgets of the big secular operations. Most Catholic and some Protestant radio and television ministries are listener- or viewer-supported. They live or die based on donations from concerned believers. I know firsthand that financial support is crucial. Prayer, of course, is always essential if we want to claim the media for Christ. Pray for both the Christian and secular media. Pray that Christian media outlets will continue to grow and that more members of the secular media will cover the moral issues of the day in a balanced manner.

Being media savvy may require stepping out of your comfort zone in order to make a difference. In Matthew's gospel, we read about Peter, who was out on the sea fishing with some of the other apostles when he spotted Jesus on the shore. Out of zeal for the Lord, he actually stepped out of the boat and began to walk across the water. A few moments later, when he realized what he was doing, he panicked and began to sink. Just then, Jesus held out his hand and supported Peter (see Matthew 14:22–33). The Gospel story speaks a mighty truth to those of us who want to fashion a better world. We see a seemingly impossible task in front of us, actually changing the output and influence of the media in our world, and we begin to sink with fear and worry. At moments like these, we should reach out for the Lord. He is always there to support us. He will be there to lead us to the sure footing we desire. From this solid ground, we then can begin to carry out our mission—a mission that will restore the true, good, and beautiful in a world that is in great need.

I look forward to joining you in the challenge.

Notes

1 "Verizon Wireless Goes Prime Time with TV Simulcasts, Via Cell Phone," *USA Today*, January 8, 2007

2 "Beyond Primetime, Will Media Grow Healthier Kids?" Common Sense Media, www.commonsensemedia.org

3 "Dying to Entertain," Parents Television Council, January 10, 2007

4 "Childhood Exposure to Media Violence Predicts Young Adult Aggressive Behavior," University of Michigan study, *Developmental Psychology*, March 2003

5 A.C. Huston and J.C. Wright, University of Kansas, "Television and the Socialization of Young Children," 1996

6 National Council on Sexual Addiction and Compulsivity, October 19, 2000, www.ncsac.org

7 *Metro Source* News Service, January 5, 2007

8 Pope John Paul II, World Communications Day 2004, "The Media and the Family: A Risk and a Richness," May 23, 2004

9 U.S. Census Bureau, *Statistical Abstract of the United States: 2007*, December 15, 2006

10 "AAP Discourages TV for Very Young Children," *Pediatrics*, August 2, 1999

11 Ibid.

12 Ibid.

13 Federal Trade Commission, "Marketing Violent Entertainment to Children," September 2000

14 *Pediatrics*, Vol. 108, No. 5, November 2001

15 Kaiser Family Foundation, www.kff.org

16 Federal Trade Commission, "Marketing Violent Entertainment to Children," September 2000

17 American Medical Association, March 8, 2006, www.ama-assn.org

18 *Washington Post*, May 19, 1999

19 Blessed Teresa of Calcutta, "Willing Slaves to the Will of God," *A Gift for God* (San Francisco: HarperSanFrancisco, 1979)

20 Thomas Paine (1737–1809), American political philosopher and author of *Common Sense*, which advocated American independence from Great Britain

21 Socrates (470–399 BC), as quoted by Plato (427–347 BC) in *The Apology*, 38a

22 "Childhood Pastimes Are Increasingly Moving Indoors," *USA Today*, July 12, 2005

23 "Are Kids Too Wired for Their Own Good," *Time*, March 27, 2006

24 Ibid.

25 "The Importance of Family Dinners II," National Center on Addiction and Substance Abuse, Columbia University, September 2005

26 Sandra Miesel, as interviewed by the author on *Catholic Connection*, Ave Maria Radio, April 2006

27 National Geographic Channel, June 2005

28 Pursuant Inc., May 2006

29 Roper for *National Geographic*, May 2006

30 Ibid.

31 "Short Attention Span Linked to TV," *USA Today*, April 5, 2004

32 "The Importance of Family Dinners II," National Center on Addiction and Substance Abuse, Columbia University, September 2005

33 Nielsen Media Research, September 2005

34 Americans for Divorce Reform, www.divorcereform.org, 2005

35 Pope John Paul II, World Communications Day 2004, "The Media and the Family: A Risk and A Richness," May 23, 2004

36 www.eating-disorder-information.com/mediacelebrities.asp

37 www.anred.com/stats.html

38 "Eating Disorders Increasing Among Children," Remuda Ranch Children's Program, PR Newswire, June 27, 2006

39 www.anred.com/stats.html

40 Institute of Medicine of the National Academies of Science, September 30, 2004, www.iom.edu

41 Annenberg Public Policy Center, *Media in the Home 1999: The Fourth Annual Survey of Parents and Children,* June 28, 1999, www.annenbergpublicpolicycenter.org

42 *Archives of Pediatric and Adolescent Medicine*, March 15, 2001

43 *International Journal of Obesity*, September 12, 2006

44 "Dying to Entertain," Parents Television Council, January 10, 2007

45 Ibid.

46 American Psychiatric Association, www.healthyminds.org

47 American Academy of Pediatrics, Policy Statement, January 2002

48 Parents Television Council, "Media Quotes," www.parentstv.org

49 "Wolves in Sheep's Clothing: A Content Analysis of Children's Television," Parents Television Council, March 2, 2006

50 "New PTC Study Finds More Violence on Children's TV Than on Adult-Oriented TV," Parents Television Council, March 2, 2006

51 "Wolves in Sheep's Clothing: A Content Analysis of Children's Television," Parents Television Council, March 2, 2006

52 Kaiser Family Foundation, *The Media Family: Electronic Media in the Lives of Infants, Toddlers, Preschoolers, and Their Parents*, May 2006

53 Ibid.

54 Ibid.

55 "Rand Study Finds Adolescents Who Watch A Lot of TV with Sexual Content Have Sex Sooner," Rand Corporation, September 7, 2004, www.rand.org

56 Ibid.

57 Statistics from Parents Television Council, www.parentstv.org

58 National Youth Risk Behavior Survey, 2005

59 *Inter Mirifica,* Decree on the Means of Social Communication (1963), No. 21

60 S. Liliana Escobar-Chavez, University of Texas Health Center and the Medical Institute for Sexual Health, *Journal of Pediatrics*, July 2005

61 Richard A. Viguerie and David Frank, *America's Right Turn: How Conservatives Used New and Alternative Media to Take Power* (Los Angeles: Bonus Books, 2004)

62 Ibid.

63 Gallup International, November 2003

64 Pope John Paul II , *The Media and the New Millennium*, Address to Members of the Central Committee for the Preparation for the Great Jubilee Year 2000

65 Ibid.

66 *Metro Parent* magazine, Ferndale, Michigan, August 2006

67 Testimony before House Committee on Energy and Commerce, April 4, 2006

68 Bishop Paul S. Leverde, "Bought with a Price: Pornography and the Attack on the Living Temple of God," November 2006

69 "The Internet Now Seen as #1 Media Concern for Parents," Common Sense Media, June 2006, www.commonsensemedia. org

70 Ibid.

71 "Teens and Technology: Youth Are Leading the Transition to a Fully Wired and Mobile Nation," July 27, 2005, Pew Internet & American Life Project

72 "Generation M: Media in the Lives of 8 to 18 Year Olds," Kaiser Family Foundation, March 9, 2005

73 National Center for Missing and Exploited Children, www.ncmec.org

74 "Generation M: Media in the Lives of 8 to 18 Year Olds," Kaiser Family Foundation, March 9, 2005

75 "Computer Experts Learn Tough Lessons about Internet Dangers," *Macomb Daily*, September 5, 2003

76 Ken Henderson, www.trueknights.org

77 Ibid.

78 USCCB statement, November 15, 2006

79 National Coalition for the Protection of Children and Families, www.nationalcoaliton.org

80 Ibid.

81 "How Many Porn Addicts Are in Your Church?" www.crosswalk.com

82 John Paul II, World Communications Day 2002, May 12, 2002

83 "Screen Time Harms School Time," Albert Einstein College, November 2006

84 "Young Teens Create Internet Subculture, Schoolwork Suffers," *Macomb Daily*, April 17, 2005

85 "Teenage Life OnLine," Jupiter Research, 2003

86 "The Church Must Learn to Cope with The Computer Culture," Statement Issued in Connection with World Communications Day 1989, May 27, 1989, No. 6

87 Ibid., No. 4

88 "Rap Listeners Prone to Alcohol, Drugs, and Violence," Pacific Institute for Research and Evaluation, April 2006

89 Ibid.

90 "MTV Smut Peddlers: Targeting Kids with Sex, Drugs, and Alcohol," Parents Television Council, March 2004

91 Ibid.

92 "Women's Magazine Urges Readers to Take Back the Music," *Macomb Daily*, January 27, 2005

93 Federal Trade Commission, Report to Congress, *Marketing Violent Entertainment to Children: A Six Month Follow-Up Review of Industry Practices in the Motion Picture, Music Recording, and Electronic Game Industries*, April 2001

94 Barna Research Group Church Attendance Survey, 2005, www.barna.org

95 National Institute on Media and the Family, "Media Violence as a Risk Factor for Children," May 2004, www.mediafamily.org

96 Ibid.

97 Ibid.

98 Teenage Research Unlimited, www.teenreseaerch.com

99 *Broadcasting and Cable*, March 7, 2005

100 *Communio et Progressio*, Pastoral Instruction on the Means of Social Communication, Written by Order of the Second Vatican Council, May 23, 1971, No. 61

101 National Easting Disorders Association, www.nationaleatingdisorders.org

102 *Health*, April 2002

103 "The Real Truth About Beauty: A Global Report," commissioned by Dove, September 2004

104 "The Plastic Surgery Epidemic: Why Teens Are Getting Botox and Breast Implants," *Family Circle*, February 2006

105 "Alcohol Use and Abuse: A Pediatric Concern, Committee on Substance Abuse," American Academy of Pediatrics, July 2001

106 Ibid.

107 Center for Science in the Public Interest, www.cspinet.org

108 Ibid.

109 "Still Growing After All These Years: Youth Exposure to Alcohol Advertising on TV," 2001-2005, December 20, 2006

110 Center on Alcohol Marketing to Youth, December 20, 2006

111 "CDC Reports Binge Drinking Is Common Among High School Students and Tied to Other Risky Behaviors," January 2, 2007, Centers for Disease Control and Prevention

112 Federal Trade Commission, www.ftc.gov

113 American Cancer Society, "Facts about Kids and Tobacco," www.cancer.org

114 "Marketing Violent Entertainment to Children: A Fourth Follow Up Review of Industry Practices in the Motion Picture, Music, Recording, and Electronic Game Industries," July 2004

115 Ibid.

116 "Girl Pleads to Retailer for Modest Clothing," May 22, 2004, www.worldnetdaily.com

117 Teen Research Unlimited, www.teenresearch.com

118 "For Many Americans, It's Time to Go On a Financial Diet," *USA Today*, April 15, 2005

119 "Was Forced Adoption Worse than Abortion?" *Detroit News*, December 27, 2006. This series of stories was written by a

columnist who, in previous articles, was explicit about her support for abortion. The series focused on several women who, prior to *Roe v. Wade*, said they were forced to place their babies for adoption. They told heart-breaking stories of the pain of imagining what their children might look like today and wondering if they were OK. All of these stories had an underlying pro-abortion theme, suggesting that the pain of "forced adoption" somehow legitimizes abortion. Interestingly, most of the statistics on adoption and pregnancy cited by the author were *pre*-1973, the year of *Roe v. Wade*. Pro-life readers raised an obvious question that was never considered by the series' author: "Would these same women, who obviously missed their children terribly and worried about their well being, feel better today if they had killed them through abortion?"

120 "Mid-Term Coverage is Bad for GOP," Center for Media and Public Affairs, October 31, 2006

121 "Media Dismiss Insult as Mistake, Hope Issue Will Vanish for Elections," Media Research Center, November 1, 2006

122 Ibid.

123 John Paul II, Address to Media, 1979

124 Media Research Center, "Cyber Alert, Since Memo ABC Does Twice as Many Fact Checks on Bush as Kerry

125 Ibid.

126 Campaign 2004, How the Media Covered the Presidential Campaign During Summer 2004

127 Bernard Goldberg, *Arrogance: Rescuing America from the Media Elite* (New York: Warner Books, 2003)

128 Such changes, though, have apparently not been sufficient to prevent reporters from fabricating stories. In November 2006, the *New York Times* faced yet another scandal when LifeSiteNews.com uncovered that a reporter writing about the pro-life movement in El Salvador (where abortion is illegal) lied about the woman in his story. The *Times* reporter, whose piece was published in the *Times* magazine, focused on an eighteen-year-old girl he claimed was serving a thirty-year prison sentence for having an abortion. As LifeSiteNews.com revealed, "The only problem with the story was that the woman was found guilty of strangling her full-term baby shortly after her birth." While the *Times* editor admitted that the reporter did not do his homework or take a fair approach to the story, the editor

of the magazine has refused to issue a correction. ("New York Times Caught in Abortion Promoting Whopper — Infanticide Portrayed as Abortion, November 28, 2006. www.LifeSiteNews. com)

129 Gallup, "Media Credibility Reaches Lowest Point in Three Decades," September 23, 2004, www.gallup.com

130 Ibid.

131 Ibid.

132 This bias not only permeates news coverage but is carried through to entertainment programming as well. A December 2006 Parents Television Council study, "Faith in a Box 2005–2006," found that religious content on television decreased, with half as many portrayals of religion during the 2005–2006 TV season than in 2003–2004. When religious themes are featured, negative depictions of religion outweigh positive ones, thirty-five percent to thirty-four percent ("Faith in a Box 2005-2006," Parents Television Council, December 14, 2006).

133 "Autopsy Issue Part of a Day of Sparring," *St. Petersburg Times*, March 30, 2005

134 "Slanting the News Against Terri Schiavo," Media Research Center, March 25, 2005

135 Ibid.

136 Zenit News Agency, April 2005, www.zenit.org

137 Top Global Media Stories for 2005, The Global Language Monitor, www.languagemonitor.com

138 Zenit News Agency, April 2005, www.zenit.org

139 "The Life of John Paul II: Shepherd of Souls or Antiquated Authoritarian?" Media Research Center, April 14, 2005

140 *CBS Early Show*, April 19, 2005

141 Vanessa Denha-Garmo, Editor, *Chaldean News*, May 2005

142 "The Trashing of the Christ: Contrast in Media Treatment of *The Da Vinci Code* and *The Passion*," Media Research Center, May 23, 2006

143 Ibid.

144 Ibid.

145 S. Robert Lichter, Linda Lichter, & Stanley Rothman, *The Media Elite*, 1986

146 *Los Angeles Times* poll, 1985

147 "Partners and Adversaries: The Contentious Connection Between Congress and the Media," Elaine Povich for the Freedom Forum, April 1996

148 John Paul II, "Media at the Service of Authentic Peace," Papal Message for World Communications Day 2003, January 24, 2003, No. 3

149 "Out of Balance: Poynter Survey Reveals Journalists' Pressure Points," Poynter Institute for Media Coverage, February 24, 2005, www.poynter.org

150 John Paul II, United Nations Address to Journalists, 1979

151 ABC News, *World News Sunday*, January 7, 2007

152 *Los Angeles Times,* January 8, 2007

153 Joe Cell, Fidelis president, as interviewed by the author on Ave Maria Radio's *Catholic Connection,* January 10, 2007

154 National Institute on Media and the Family, "Children and Family Fact Sheet," www.mediafamily.org

155 "The Media Family: Electronic Media in the Lives of Infants, Toddlers, Preschoolers, and Their Parents," Kaiser Family Foundation, May 24, 2006

156 William Donahue, *Catalyst,* Catholic League for Religious and Civil Rights, July 25, 2006, www.catholicleague.org

157 "The Media Family: Electronic Media in the Lives of Infants, Toddlers, Preschoolers, and Their Parents," Kaiser Family Foundation, May 24, 2006

158 "A Lot Easier Said Than Done; Parents Talk About Raising Children in Today's America," Public Agenda, October 2002

159 "President Signs the Broadcast Decency Enforcement Act of 2005," June 15, 2006

160 John Paul II, as quoted on CNN, April 6, 2005

Index

Your Family Media Guide

Alternative News Sources

Cable Networks

Eternal Word Television Network (EWTN)
www.ewtn.com
5817 Old Leeds Road
Irondale, AL 35210
(205) 271-2900

FOX News Channel
www.foxnews.com
1211 Avenue of the Americas
New York, NY 10036
(212) 301-3000
1-888-369-4762

Radio Networks

Ave Maria Radio
www.avemariaradio.net
www.mycatholicradio.com
One Ave Maria Drive
P.O. Box 504
Ann Arbor, MI 48106
(734) 930-5200

EWTN Global Catholic Radio
www.ewtn.com
5817 Old Leeds Road
Irondale, AL 35210
(205) 271-2900

Relevant Radio
www.relevantradio.com
P.O. Box 10707
Green Bay, WI 54307-0707
(920) 469-3021

Talk Radio Network
www.talkradionetwork.com
P.O. Box 3755
Central Point, OR 97502
(541) 664-8827

Internet

Catholic Culture
www.catholicculture.com

Catholic World News
www.cwnews.com

NewsMax
www.newsmax.com

Worldnet Daily
www.worldnetdaily.com

Washington Times
www.washingtontimes.com

Broadcast Television Networks

ABC (owned by Walt Disney Company)
www.abc.com
500 S. Buena Vista Street
Burbank, CA 91521
(818) 560-1000

ABC News
www.abcnews.com
77 West 66th Street
New York, NY 10023
(212) 456-7777

CBS (owned by CBS
Corporation)
www.cbs.com
51 West 52nd Street
New York, NY 10019
(212) 975-4321

CBS News
www.cbsnews.com
555 West 57th Street
New York, NY 10019
(212) 975-4114

The CW (co-owned by CBS and
Time Warner)
www.cwtv.com
11800 Wilshire Blvd.
Los Angeles, CA 90025
(310) 575-7000

FOX (owned by News
Corporation)
www.fox.com
P.O. Box 900
Beverly Hills, CA 90213
(310) 369-1000

NBC (owned by NBC Universal,
a unit of General Electric)
www.nbc.com
30 Rockefeller Plaza
New York, NY 10112
(212) 664-4444

**Public Broadcasting Service
(PBS)**
www.pbs.org
2100 Crystal Drive
Arlington, VA 22202

Cable Networks

ABC Family Channel (owned
by Walt Disney Company)
www.abcfamily.com
3800 West Alameda Avenue
Burbank, CA 91505
(818) 560-1000

**A&E Networks / History
Channel** (co-owned by Hearst
Corporation, NBC Universal,
and Walt Disney Company)
www.aetv.com
235 East 45th Street
New York, NY 10017
(212) 210-1400

Comedy Central
www.comedycentral.com
1775 Broadway
New York, NY 10019
(212) 767-8600

Court TV
www.courttv.com
600 Third Avenue, 2nd Floor
New York, NY 10016
(212) 973-2800

CNBC (owned by NBC
Universal)
www.cnbc.com
900 Sylvan Avenue
Englewood Cliffs, NJ 07632
(201) 585-2622

CNN (owned by Time Warner)
One CNN Center
Box 105366
Atlanta, GA 30303-5366
(404) 827-1500

Discovery Channel / The Learning Channel (TLC)
www.discovery.com;
www.tlc.com
One Discovery Place
Silver Spring, MD 20910-3354
(240) 662-2000

Disney Channel (owned by Walt Disney Company)
www.disneychannel.com
3800 West Alameda Avenue
Burbank, CA 91505
(818) 569-7500

E! Entertainment Television
www.eonline.com
5750 Wilshire Boulevard
Los Angeles, CA 90036–3709
(323) 954-2400

ESPN (owned by Walt Disney Company)
www.espn.com
ESPN Plaza
Bristol, CT 06010-9454
(860) 766-2000

HBO / Cinemax (owned by Time Warner)
www.hbo.com;
www.cinemax.com
1100 Avenue of the Americas
New York, NY 10036
(212) 512-1000

Lifetime Television (co-owned by Walt Disney Company and Hearst Corporation)
www.lifetimetv.com
309 W. 49th Street
New York, NY 10019
(212) 424-7293

MSNBC (co-owned by NBC Universal and Microsoft)
www.msnbc.com
One MSNBC Plaza
Secaucus, NJ 07094
(201) 583-5000

MTV / VH1 (owned by Viacom)
www.mtv.com; www.vh1.com
1515 Broadway
New York, NY 10036
(212) 258-6000

Nickelodeon (owned by Viacom)
www.nick.com
1515 Broadway
New York, NY 10036
(212) 258-8000

Oxygen Media
www.oxygen.com
75 9th Avenue, 7th Floor
New York, NY 10011
(212) 651-2070

Sci-Fi Channel (owned by NBC Universal)
www.scifi.com
30 Rockefeller Plaza
New York, NY 10112
(212) 664-4444

Spike TV (owned by Viacom)
www.spiketv.com
1775 Broadway
New York, NY 10019
(212) 767-8705

TBS / TNT (owned by Time
Warner)
www.tbs.tv; www.tnt.tv
1050 Techwood Drive, NW
Atlanta, GA 30318
(404) 885-4339

USA Network (owned by NBC
Universal)
www.usanetwork.com
30 Rockefeller Plaza
New York, NY 10112
(212) 664-4444

Media Research, Influence, and Activism

Accuracy in Media (AIM)
www.aim.org
4455 Connecticut Avenue, NW
Suite #330
Washington, DC 20008
(202) 364-4401
1-800-787-4567

American Academy of Pediatrics (AAP)
www.aap.org
141 Northwest Point Boulevard
Elk Grove Village, IL 60007-1098
(847) 434–4000

American Family Association
www.afa.net
P.O. Drawer 2440
Tupelo, MS 38803
(662) 844-5036

Center for Media and Public Affairs
www.cmpa.com
2100 L Street, NW, Suite 300
Washington, DC 20037
(202) 223-2942
(202) 872-4014

Concerned Women for America
www.cwfa.org
1015 Fifteenth St., NW, Suite 1100
Washington, DC 20005
(202) 488-7000

Family Research Council
www.frc.org
801 G Street, NW
Washington, DC 20001
(202) 393-2100

Focus on the Family
www.family.org
Colorado Springs, CO 80995
(719) 531-5181

Media Research Center
www.mrc.org
325 S. Patrick Street
Alexandria, VA 22314
(703) 683-9733

Morality in Media
www.moralityinmedia.org
475 Riverside Drive, Suite 239
New York, NY 10115
(212) 870-3222

National Center for Missing and Exploited Children
www.ncmec.org
699 Prince Street
Alexandria, VA 22314-3175
(703) 274-3900

National Coalition for the Protection of Children and Families
www.nationalcoalition.org
800 Compton Road, Suite 9224
Cincinnati, OH 45231
(513) 521-6337

National Institute for Media and the Family
www.mediafamily.org
606 24th Avenue South, Suite 606
Minneapolis, MN 55454
(888) 672-KIDS

Parents Television Council
www.parentstv.org
707 Wilshire Boulevard, #2075
Los Angeles, CA 90017
(213) 629-9255

Renewing the Mind of the Media
www.renewingmedia.org
United States Conference of Catholic Bishops (USCCB)
3211 4th Street, NE
Washington DC 20017-1194
(202) 541-3000

True Knights
www.trueknights.org
P.O. Box 3113
Broken Arrow, OK 74013-3113
(800) 950-2008

Movie, Music, and Video Game Resources

Decent Films
www.decentfilms.com

Entertainment Software Ratings Board
www.esrb.org

Grading the Movies
www.grading.movies.com

Kids In Mind
www.kids-in-mind.com

Lyrics.Com
www.lyrics.com

Internet Filters
www.cleanweb.net
www.covenanteyes.com
www.family.net
www.mayberry.net
www.truevine.net

About the Author

Teresa Tomeo is a veteran broadcast journalist with more than twenty years of experience as a radio and television news reporter and anchorperson, mainly in the Detroit area. First working as an award-winning radio reporter and news anchor, Teresa received recognition for her work from the Associated Press, the Detroit Press Club, and American Women in Radio and Television.

After making the move to television news in 1988, she worked as a reporter and anchor for WKBD-TV, and later reported for Detroit's ABC affiliate, WXYZ-TV. Her assignments at WXYZ took her across the country covering some of the most significant stories of the 1990s, including the Oklahoma City bombing and the Pope John Paul II's 1995 visit to United States.

Despite her success and recognition, Teresa become disillusioned by media trends toward sensationalism, violence, and liberal bias. She is now a professional speaker, media consultant, and host of the *Catholic Connection*, heard daily on Ave Maria Radio and distributed nationally by EWTN and Sirius Satellite Radio.

Rome. Mecca.
What's the difference?

Inside Islam: A Guide for Catholics utilizes a popular question-and-answer format so that all Catholics–both the theological novice and the well-catechized–can learn the basics of Islam. ***Inside Islam*** is an essential resource for anyone who wants to know more about this troubling faith from the Middle East, including:

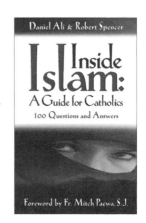

- The Islamic view of God and its dramatic implications
- The role of Jesus in Islamic theology
- Why Islamic theology can breed terrorist activity
- Islam's controversial theology of *jihad,* or "holy war"
- Why anti-Semitic texts in the Koran seriously strain Jewish-Islamic relations
- How the Koran and other Islamic writings directly contradict what God has revealed in the Old and New Testaments
- How Islamic theology undermines the inherent dignity of the human person
- Why women in many Islamic countries are denied basic human rights

www.AscensionPress.com • 800-376-0520

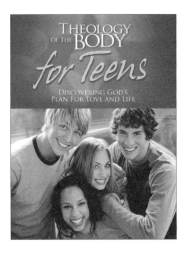

Sample Media Privilege Cards

Ryan **:30** TV Priviledge	Ryan **:30** IPOD Time
Ryan **:20** TV Priviledge	Ryan **:20** IPOD Time
Ryan **:15** TV Priviledge	Ryan **:15** IPOD Time
Ryan **:10** TV Priviledge	Ryan **:10** IPOD Time